How to Grow

Nurture Your Garden, Nurture Yourself

Marcus Bridgewater

HarperOne

An Imprint of HarperCollinsPublishers

HarperCollins books may be purchased for educational, business, or sales promotional use. For information, please email the Special Markets Department at SPsales@harpercollins.com.

FIRST EDITION

Designed by SBI Book Arts, LLC
Illustrations by Valenty/Shutterstock

Library of Congress Cataloging-in-Publication Data has been applied for.

ISBN 978-0-06-314144-5

22 23 24 25 26   LSC   10 9 8 7 6 5 4 3 2 1

This collection of thoughts and words
is dedicated to all those who strive to grow.
This message is for those who desire inspiration
but feel disconnected from *Life*. The ideas are for
those who are determined to make change and
are willing to challenge themselves to do so.
These techniques are dedicated to my experiences:
painful, essential, and rewarding. The book
is dedicated to the future: May you be
filled with peace, balance, and harmony
among all living things.

CONTENTS

Contents

How to Grow

Introduction

Living in a Thorny Rosebush

I grew up in farm country, and while we were rich in spirit and nature, we were poor in resources and assets. It was a beautiful place with flowers and orange groves and cornfields. I had trees to climb, woods to explore, and railroads to walk. I also had the love of my grandma, the matriarch of the small town of Zellwood, Florida. She's now the oldest person living in the area. It was here, in her garden, that I began learning about plant care as a four-year-old boy.

Some of my earliest memories are of watering the hibiscus trees, picking their red and pink flowers, and chewing on the stems. I learned about the importance of watering at the roots when the sun was hot, and the need to be consistent in my care of the garden. Paying diligent attention to the plants was essential to their growth. Most importantly, I learned that growth cannot be forced, only fostered.

Alongside these joys, the thorny rosebush pricked me too. Zellwood was changing, as drugs, violence, and crime crept in from the cities. I was bullied at school for having a speech impediment, challenged as the only child who looked like me in the gifted class, and laughed at for being sickly and losing my hair. As I grew into an adult I learned the importance of carrying those early lessons with me and turning them to positive ends. I found ways to apply my life experiences to keeping my plants alive and found that I began to thrive, and so did my plants.

Nature provides me with connection, a sense of belonging, and peace. I spend as much time as I can outside cherishing the delights and wonders of my plants. When people spend too much time looking at screens, they disconnect themselves from the life all around them. Spending time with our hands in the dirt gives us the opportunity to feel the warmth of the sun and the coolness of the wind and to experience the clarity that comes with fresh air. With something different to appreciate in every plant, our senses are stimulated and engaged. The vibrant colors of blooming flowers are a gorgeous sight for our eyes, and the smell of fresh nectar makes every moment in the garden sweet. The sound of leaves rustling with the swaying of the trees and the songs of the birds who nest in them remind us we are never alone when we are outside. Food almost always tastes better when you grow it yourself. When the seasons change, our plants adapt and take on new forms, reminding us that we are constantly in motion. We are never done working, learning, and growing, and there is joy to be found in every seed we plant.

I posted my first video that connected plants to people online at the suggestion of a former student and friend. He believed people were hungry for guidance on growth and wellness and would embrace my garden observations and "wisdom." I barely understood social media at the time but within a few weeks, I'd been compared to Mr. Rogers and Bob Ross more times than I could count and found a community of people yearning to grow.

Although I still have much to learn, I'm proud and humbled that so many people are interested in my message. I hope this book helps you find peace in your mind, balance in your body, and harmony in your spirit. Perhaps you'll be inspired to get a plant or start a garden or to care for the greenery you have in new ways. Either way, let's reconnect with nature and grow together.

A New Beginning

In my twenty-seventh year, I started working at a private preparatory school in Texas, a job I saw as an opportunity to nurture, empower, and share skills that will last a lifetime.

This job made me do something I hadn't done before: settle. I bought a house and committed to living in one place after years of traveling every few months. The adjustment was difficult, but I did my best to find ways to adapt. At the same time, my dear friend's mother closed her nursery and had a surplus of leftover plants. She gave me sixteen exotic plants as a housewarming gift and I drove them from Florida to my new home in Texas before the start of my second school year. Within two months, I'd killed nine.

I was determined to keep the rest alive. For the first time in years, I was reconnected to those days as a child in my grandmother's garden, the place that holds my earliest memories of watering the hibiscus trees, picking their red and pink flowers and, as I mentioned, chewing on the stems. Plant care was new territory for me as an adult, but I was committed to learning everything I could to save the others. I went to the local plant stores and bought hundreds of dying and marked-down plants—some cost as little as six cents. I didn't care what they were, and their names were unimportant to me. All I wanted was to help them grow.

Not only did I learn how to encourage growth and keep my plants healthy, but I found parallels between plants and people. Like plants, we need resources to grow. We go through different stages of growth. Our environment and community affect our growth. We maximize our potential when presented with the right conditions. Above all, the *Life* inside us yearns to grow. With care and attention, we can cultivate that growth.

The primary difference between us and our plants is that we must *choose* to focus on our growth. Plants do it instinctively. We can consider our environment, evaluate our community, and assess what we need to do to best support our mental health, physical fitness, and spiritual awareness. We can also ignore all the factors that affect our growth. Unlike plants, we are liable to become distracted and shift our focus away from our growth. Our agency can be a tool or a vice; it's up to us.

These parallels I saw reinforced conclusions I'd drawn from my observations in my studies and travels. It was an enlightening epiphany, to realize we can learn about ourselves by learning about plants. I brought these lessons to my classroom and watched my students prosper. I developed stronger bonds with my family and friends. I felt more grounded and at peace.

In the midst of my learning and experimenting with plants, one lesson changed how I would forever think about growth: *We cannot* make *anything grow, but we can foster environments where* Life *wants to grow.* Growth cannot be forced, only nurtured. As much as I wanted to see every plant in my care flourish, I recognized this would only happen if I paid attention, considered the factors that affect growth, and fostered the right conditions. It later dawned on me that I did for my plants what I'd done for myself all my life.

Reflecting on Growth

Spending time in the garden slowed me down, enabling me to reflect on my past, my experience, and the lessons I'd learned along the way. I thought about the challenges I'd overcome, and how I managed to confront difficulty time and time again. I saw myself in the discount and dying plants I'd rescue and nurture back to life and felt fortunate to have maintained the motivation to keep moving forward.

Why shouldn't I give up? In my lifetime, students, peers, and family alike have asked me this question in the face of adversity too many times to ignore. I've seen an absence of motivation in people who feel their lives lack a purpose, as well as in those who feel isolated, disconnected, alone, or overwhelmed when confronting adversity. There have been times in my own life when challenges were so great that I questioned my purpose and wondered why I should persevere. I've come to believe that our purpose is an opportunity, an opportunity to grow. Pursuing a lifetime of growth gives us the best chance of developing and maintaining a quality well-being as well as cultivating strong communities. Rejecting growth is depressing, unproductive, destructive, and unrewarding. Without growth, we regress, and move further from life and closer to death.

Although maintaining one's determination toward growth takes continuous effort, I say it is worth it. Like plants, we don't flower unless we grow. Like plants, we only flower when the conditions are right. Giving up too soon and forsaking growth means we compromise our potential and may never know what we are capable of. We don't know what heights our leaves could reach, what colors our petals could bloom, or how we may contribute to the overall vibrance of a garden.

It's important to remember that we are not alone. We

affect those around us the same way creatures and plants in a garden come together as an ecosystem. If one plant develops an infestation that goes unaddressed, the entire garden is liable to fall. When we all focus on growth, we grow together and foster environments where communities can thrive. We benefit from the resource of community that supports and nurtures our growth as we contribute to the greater good of our gardens.

I remind my students, peers, and family that it's never too late to start focusing on growth. I've cared for plants that lay dormant for months until the conditions were what they needed to reveal a sprout of green. I tell them to focus on themselves because we all grow at different rates. I once placed two silver satin pothos three feet from each other on the same ledge; within a year, one grew vines five feet in length that trail to the ground while the other's vines are barely ten inches long. Both plants are treasures to me—one is just situated closer to a window. I had one student who was desperate to grow into the person he wanted to be; I pointed out that growth happens in stages, and the process isn't complete without every stage. He learned to appreciate the process and grew into an incredible young man over the course of a few years. He came to see that he could not force his growth, he could only foster it—and fostering takes time.

I'm not an expert gardener. I have no formal training in botany, horticulture, or agriculture. I grew my garden out of a penchant for learning and a passion for watching things grow, and in observing my plants, I learned ways to help people grow, too.

Learning from Nature

Plants do not grow longer vines, more leaves, or taller stems without more roots forming beneath the soil. We cannot sustain our growth unless we grow in all parts of ourselves, too: our mental health, physical fitness, and spiritual awareness. These are the three tenets of growth that I invite you to nurture in this book. To work on the mind yet ignore the body is to limit oneself and create imbalance. Trying to flex our spiritual awareness without considering our mental health will make it harder to appreciate and cultivate the power of community. We must work on all the elements of our well-being to truly grow.

A strong mind, body, and spirit yields individuals who are capable, resilient, kind, patient, and positive. But it can be daunting to embark on this journey. We might get in the way of our own growth without realizing it. Frustration with a perceived lack of progress, comparing ourselves to others, or feeling stuck can lead us to view ourselves harshly. *Assessment Versus Judgment* is a dichotomy that helps me remain objective and conscious of how I think about something (see the next section for the five foundational dichotomies I use as tools for growth). An *assessment* is a temporary conclusion we draw from analysis and it can change with continued observation. A *judgment* is a final conclusion we draw from an analysis that does *not* change because we stop observing. In our evaluation of our well-being, we should aim to make assessments with objectivity and clarity.

I don't believe people who tell me they have a "black thumb." The chances are high that these people simply haven't practiced enough. Don't limit yourself with such thinking. If you've been led to believe growth is impossible for you, it's time to rethink your potential. As we continue, let's challenge ourselves and question our perceptions and any judgments we have made about our mental, physical, and spiritual well-being.

A Foundation for Growth

After years of traveling, writing, and learning, I concluded that the best way to grow is to focus on our mind, body, and spirit. I took every opportunity to meet and learn from spiritual elders and leaders along the way, and their lessons corroborated my observation. As I considered this topic further, I realized our understanding of these ancient terms has evolved to fit our modern language. The betterment of our mind, body, and spirit lies in how we govern our mental health, physical fitness, and spiritual awareness.

I used my writing and notes to create resources for myself that would help me achieve my goal of making positive and productive choices—choices that forward my growth. Among these resources are my *Choice Dichotomies*, tools I developed to consider the different ways I can approach a situation. These thought tools guide me toward making choices that support my well-being.

Just as we need tools to garden, we need tools to align ourselves with wellness and growth. My Choice Dichotomies are like the seed, soil, shovel, and moisture meter we'd utilize to start a garden, and we'll use them to cultivate growth within ourselves. The final dichotomy refers to the garden itself as well as our role in it.

I'm committed to making choices aligned with maintaining my well-being and aiding my growth, and avoiding choices that compromise my well-being or stunt my growth. We will explore different dichotomies and their applications throughout this book but there are five that create a foundation of understanding the others. Let's think of these Choice Dichotomies as supplies for our personal toolbox. Anyone can start a project, be it a garden or personal growth, with the right tools.

A Seed: Choice and Experience

Every choice we make influences our experience, and I want my experience to reflect a quality well-being and trajectory for growth. My dichotomy *Choice and Experience* refers to the "cause and effect" of our lives: *choice* is our *cause*, and our *experience* is our *effect*. Our choices are seeds that grow into the plants of our experience. Let's consider every choice we make as if it were a seed planted in our gardens—carefully and intentionally.

Soil: Community and Environment

Making positive choices is much easier when we're part of a community and environment that encourage our growth. We need nurture and support, just like the seeds we plant. The soil and conditions are important to the sprouting of the seed.

Community and Environment explains the two main factors that affect our growth.

Community refers to *who* we grow with, and our *environment* is *where* we grow. To maximize my growth and keep myself on a path forward, I want to be part of a community that supports me and an environment that fosters prosperity.

Moisture Meter:
Perspective Versus Perception

It can be difficult for new gardeners to assess whether or not their plants have enough water. The moisture meter is a great tool to help us out—we can stick it in soil, and it indicates how dry or moist soil is. Planting a seed in soil is the way to start gardening, but the process doesn't end there. We need to monitor the plant and water it as needed. As we add to our plant collection, we'll need to know the hydration needs of each distinct plant if we want them to grow.

Perspective Versus Perception keeps me objective and aware that everything is more complicated than what I can see, feel, hear, touch, and taste. My *perspective* is how I see the world based on *my* collection of experiences; it is my context for understanding. Our *perception* is how we decide to interpret both the world and our experiences. We only have one perspective, but we can view it through infinite perceptions. I think of perspective as my eyes, and perception as the glasses lenses I choose to wear.

Learning the signs of hydration in a plant can take time and practice. We may look at a plant and perceive it looks thirsty while a moisture meter indicates the soil has a high moisture level. Our perception of something's experience may not be its reality, so we limit ourselves if we make assumptions.

Additionally, we can't apply one plant's moisture levels to every plant; we need to check each plant individually as all are different. I think of each plant's moisture as its perspective—utterly unique because of its conditions, state of being, position, and proximity to sunlight.

Shovel: Tool Versus Vice

While we can use our capable hands to dig holes and plant seeds, it certainly helps to have a quality shovel in our toolbox. We need care and caution when digging, though, because we don't want to dig too deep or too wide, potentially disrupting the growing roots of other plants, and we don't want to stunt the growth of our new seed by digging a hole that's larger or smaller than it needs.

Tool Versus Vice is a dichotomy I use to identify and separate productive and destructive resources. Everything on this planet is a tool—every hobby, habit, routine, device, relationship, and item. They are tools when we use them with discipline and moderation, and they encourage productivity in our lives. The moment we stop applying discipline and moderation, the tool becomes a vice.

Our shovel can be a great tool we use to efficiently dig holes for our new seeds, but if we dig at the expense of other plants or without thought, it becomes a vice. *Every individual decides for themselves if something is a tool or a vice.* We are responsible for our choices and how we use the resources at our disposal.

Life Versus the World: The Gardener and the Garden

We began as hunters and foragers, eating what we could find in the land we occupied or traveled through. There came a time when some of us decided to settle and take on the responsibility of intentionally growing plants to eat, heal, and enjoy. At this moment, these early humans became gardeners with gardens to care for.

Life *and* the World describes the phenomenon of

humans contending with the beautiful yet harsh conditions of nature and innovating to survive. Humans were born onto a planet that existed long before our arrival, and I believe the planet is governed by Life, the energy that makes the planet move, grow, and sustain all living beings. In efforts to overcome the challenges presented by Life, we developed the World. This refers to everything humans have deliberately created, like civilization, institutions, and gardens.

Institutions of the World include medicine, transportation, education, housing, and finance, all existing with the potential to improve our experience as well as our well-being—our mental health, physical fitness, and spiritual awareness. A key problem occurred when we decided to favor efficiency, the maximization of time and space, over our collective well-being and the state of the planet that sustains us. At this point, the tool that was the World became a vice, leading Life *and* the World to become Life *versus* the World.

I think of gardeners as vessels of Life, and gardens as the World. The state of the garden relies on gardeners' attentiveness and care, as well as how gardeners treat themselves. Life fuels the World the way gardeners maintain their gardens.

Life and the World should not be at odds. Treat your garden with respect and understand that growth takes time. Gardeners should not have to use poisonous pesticides on their vegetables, but if they feel pressured to save time, they may compromise, and compromise their health in turn. Speed does not necessarily equate to efficiency. Rushing often creates more problems for us to deal with, aggravating our desire to move quickly.

To preserve your well-being and the state of your garden, remember the World is a tool that you, the gardener, use to foster prosperity in your experience with Life.

From Thorns to Flowers

I don't keep up with the tally, but many people from my childhood years in Zellwood did not make it. The thorns of the rosebush are a brutal place to grow up and many never make it out, especially if they don't know to look up and press forward.

The World is complex, with an intricate web of roots leading to a maze of stalks, stems, and branches, all woven together to create the beautiful rosebush of our earth. Within the web are thousands of thorns and other nuisances that can hurt, hinder, or stunt our growth. With maturity and a desire to grow, we can choose to learn from any pain, turning the experiences into something we can appreciate. The rosebush isn't perfect, and many of us are born into places we wish we could change. My circumstances presented me with an opportunity to grow and produce my own unique flowers, and I believe the same is possible for you.

Whether you are creating a garden, bettering your well-being, or aiming to create stronger communities and healthier environments, it will take great effort, and you may not see your progress for some time. Gardening is the same: it takes regular watering, pruning, weeding, and planting. Don't let this stop you—your labor is worth it.

I'm thankful for the help I've had along the way, but I'm certain I would not be in this position if I had not prioritized my well-being and sought out ways to grow. My garden saved me from a dark period at the end of my twenties and pushed me into a new decade of unanticipated growth. In this book, I hope to share tools I've used to better my mental health, physical fitness, and spiritual awareness through lessons I've learned from my garden. We'll start with our mental health, then look at physical fitness, and finish with spiritual awareness. I'll share lessons I've learned from my garden as well as personal experiences ranging from my childhood to recent years that shaped my approach toward growth and maintaining my well-being.

I've come a long way from the first-time homeowner who didn't know a pothos from a potato ivy. I still confuse the occasional Christmas cactus with the Thanksgiving cactus, but it doesn't stop me from learning how to help each flourish and flower. I made a lot of mistakes, lost cherished plants, and felt defeated more than once. As you read this book and consider my thoughts, use them as motivation and reminders to use all experiences, joyous and difficult alike, to fuel your growth.

PART ONE

Mental Health

Cultivating Our Garden Within

H ow are you so happy?"

The first time I was asked this question, words were lost on me. Happy? I've never considered myself a happy person. The majority of my life has been spent in darkness. I never had reason to think my happiness mattered.

"How are you so happy?"

People ask me this question all the time now. In recent years, I've become more articulate in describing the difference between *happiness* and *positivity*. For me, happiness is an emotion; it's temporary, a fleeting feeling of joy or pleasure. Positivity is a mindset, which is longer lasting and more expansive. Positivity can promote happiness, but if we rely on happiness to maintain positivity, it will be that much harder for us when we lose a plant or our flowers wilt.

"How are you so positive?"

This is much easier for me to answer. I am positive because I've had to be. I never had the opportunity to rely on anyone to solve problems for me, or time to wallow. Giving up was never an option. To survive and make progress in my life, I needed to train myself to embrace challenges, appreciate every blessing, and keep moving forward.

When I lost nine out of my first sixteen plants, I faced the challenge of keeping the remaining seven alive. I was determined to learn what I did wrong with the ones I lost as well as what I did right with the survivors, and I believe my mindset pushed me to have this approach. I could have given up and let the rest die, but I wanted to learn and grow alongside the remaining plants. As I learned how to set up a healthy space for my plants, I was reminded of how fortunate I am to have a mindset focused on growth.

Nurture Positivity for Personal Growth

Developing a positive mindset takes drive, and maintaining it takes practice. I developed a positive mindset after realizing that nothing productive comes from focusing on sadness or negativity. I decided to step up and do my best to stop adversity from getting and keeping me down. Every challenge, loss, failure, and setback was an opportunity to practice positivity, and I continue practicing to this day. Through practice, I maintain my positivity. Developing a positive mindset is only the beginning; maintaining it means we can harness it long term. Like establishing any habit or routine, this process demanded discipline, commitment, and patience. Every second spent working toward this goal has proved itself worth the effort as I am now strong, confident, and capable.

I recently learned of a term—"toxic positivity." This term refers to the act of ignoring problems, pretending to be unaffected by negative situations, and dismissing one's emotions for the sake of being (or feigning to be) happy or positive. This is not at all what I mean when I promote positivity. To make progress in our lives, we need to address problems, deal with negative situations, and feel our emotions. I believe positivity is a *tool* that can help us along the way.

Imagine you have spent hours placing different plants together in a planter you plan to hang off the side of your house. Once the viny silver satin pothos, colorful bromeliads, and leafy ivy are snug in the soil, you step on a ladder to hang the planter on a nail below your roof. Just as you are about to place it on the hanger, the planter slips from your hands, causing the plants and soil to spill all over the ground.

If you handle the situation with toxic positivity, you might say, "As frustrated as I am that I dropped this planter, it is not a problem. I will think of my happy place as I throw everything away. There is no need for me to bother with gardening if it can evoke such unpleasant feelings. I will smile and try to forget this happened."

Using positivity as a *tool*, you might say, "This is frustrating. I was looking forward to finishing this project. Next time, I will make sure to use a steadier hand or ask someone for help. As disappointed as I am, I cannot leave the plants or mess here. Let me find a new home for these plants so they do not die, and use this experience as a lesson to help me be successful with future planting projects."

Positivity is the source of my mental peace. It allows me to be calm and collected. After studying and training with spiritual leaders around the world, I found that the mind is composed of three elements: *needs*, *inspiration*, and *understanding*.

Needs are the urges that come from the body and affect the mind, such as fatigue or hunger. *Inspiration* refers to the urges of the spirit and is unique to every person. Our inspirations are often considered our passions. Some of us are inspired to sing, cook, or nurture; others are driven to write, build, or run. Being disconnected from what inspires us can result in malaise, emptiness, hopelessness, frustration, and irritability. To govern our needs and inspiration, we need understanding.

Understanding is awareness of our needs and inspiration. When we understand how the body affects the mind, we are able to maintain clarity and control of ourselves. This awareness is recognizing the irritability we feel when we are hungry is the result of needing sustenance. Understanding helps us compose ourselves rather than act on that irritability and do something rash. Similarly, our passions are deeply connected to the mind. Understanding our inspirations sustains our self-motivation, which is key to maintaining our energy and positivity.

Every day, I *choose* to be positive. It is a choice I consciously and deliberately make countless times a day. When I am asked about how I got to this point, or why I am the way I am, I am honest about the time and effort I have invested in my mentality. Many people are dismissive of this and instead choose to believe I was simply "born this way." Others appreciate the direction I have steered myself in and ask if I have any insight to share with them. Anyone can develop and maintain a positive mindset, but we have to be open to putting in the work.

Personal growth is like managing a garden. The mind is the collection of seeds we plant and the roots we grow. To set our plants up for success, we need to curate and cultivate a space for growth. It takes drive and consistent maintenance, but it is possible with practice. Green thumb or not, I believe anyone can create a garden; we just need focus and systems to support growth. With the right tools, anyone can create environments where seeds want to grow.

MENTAL METAPHOR

Making a Path for Yourself

Imagine that you're in the desert surrounded by nothing but open sand. It is safe but lonely and uninspiring here. You aren't in immediate danger, but you won't grow if you stay. After hours walking in the blistering heat, you find yourself standing in front of a wall of forest and thick brush. You need to carve a way through it, which requires strong tools, stamina, planning, and attention to detail. You will also need patience and persistence.

The brush is so thick, it's hard work, even with a machete. After cutting a little way through the brush, the blade of your machete has dulled. Fortunately, you have a whetstone that you can use to sharpen it. You also notice that debris is building up, so you carry it out to the clearing. Although it takes time and energy to restore the blade's cutting edge and to remove the debris, you carefully repeat this process until you finally clear a good path for yourself.

You're now deep into the forest, with only a narrow trail behind you. You need to rest, but this is an unknown space. You are afraid, so you want to go back to the familiar desert that you know well. The easiest way out is back the way you came. But the brush keeps growing and the path behind you is threatening to close up, trapping you in the forest. You hack your way back to where you started. It takes a lot less energy and time because there's less for you to clear, and you now understand how the environment responds to your machete.

After returning to the place where the forest meets the desert, you rest. This is a safe place. But the unknown of the forest calls to you—you know something is there for you even though it requires difficult work. Then it's time to begin your next attempt to find a way through. You notice that while it's still hard, the work has gotten easier, so you can push farther forward than you did last time. But the brush always tries to reclaim the path you've cut.

This is how we feel when creating something new. Developing my positive mindset was a lot like carving out my own path. Although others had taken this journey before me and had offered wisdom, I had to embrace the challenge myself. I learned that I needed discipline, the right tools, and energy to drive forward into the unknown. The same is true for you: I can offer you my wisdom, but you must embrace the challenge yourself.

Now I understand that we are *all* that person clearing the path, while the world continues to change around us. Despite the troubles we encounter, we have to find a way to keep moving forward. We are human and we make mistakes, and sometimes our plans fail. Sometimes we have the wrong tools for what we're trying to accomplish. If that happens and we find ourselves stuck, it may be time to reach out for help.

Observation

Take Time to Look Around

Stop; take a moment to breathe and collect yourself. How do you feel? Is something pressing on your mind? Is something clouding your thoughts and focus?

It's beneficial to routinely check in with ourselves, or observe the state of our minds. Observation is the act of applying awareness to gain information, and we can use this information to make thoughtful and calculated choices. If something is weighing on my mind, I may unknowingly be annoyed or impatient with those around me, hurting my relationships. After observing that something is on my mind, I can use my *understanding* of the issue to ensure that I do not let it affect my interactions with others.

Foster an Environment for Growth

Sometimes external factors influence the mind. Maybe we are too hot and have started to get distracted, or maybe we are too cold and started to get too sleepy. Like plants, these elements of the world around us impact our well-being. The more we observe ourselves and our thoughts, and our environment, the more information we have to inform our next decision.

Awareness of your environment means acknowledging its nuances and the resources it has to offer. This is as true for us as it is for our gardens. How large or small is your future green oasis? Will you be planting in the ground outside, or filling your room with potted flowers, vines, and succulents? Do other creatures, such as birds, insects, and squirrels, share the space with you? Does your space change with the time of day? To ensure the health and longevity of your plants, you need to consider the existing ecosystem, the sunlight, and the climatic zone you're planning to garden in.

Knowing the climatic zone aids in the success of our garden. This tells us things about our seasons and times of year we are likely to see blooms. In a similar way, I have a friend who grew up in Minnesota surrounded by snow, but until she moved to Texas she said she didn't feel like she could be comfortable. Another friend felt the opposite and left Texas for the low temperature of Colorado winters. Neither of my friends felt comfortable until they moved to the conditions that supported their growth.

Learning to observe my garden before bringing new plants home taught me important lessons about self-awareness. If I want to change a habit or adjust my routine, I need to be aware of my existing patterns. Self-awareness allows me to understand why I make the choices I make and what I can do to steer myself in positive directions. We are similar to our plants in that we're also affected by the different seasons. When we know what *causes* changes in our mentality and emotions, it's far easier to be objective and clear in our thoughts.

When I was seven, I learned about the importance of awareness as well as the chaos that can result from a lack of awareness after inadvertently causing my grandmother to fall in a giant hole in her backyard.

MARCUS TALES #1
A Hole in the Yard

Palm trees rustled around me while birds called to one another in the skies high above, and twigs snapped underneath every step of my feet. Closing my eyes, I strained my ears listening for the growl or hiss of a creature that might be hiding nearby. Alone in the woods, I carefully evaluated my surroundings.

This was a typical day for me when I was five years old. Growing up in the countryside, I spent my days exploring the dense forests behind my grandmother's house. Bobcats, alligators, and rattlesnakes called the woods their home, and I ran into all of them in my childhood expeditions. I often pretended they were chasing me, forcing myself to learn the ins and outs of every tree, rock, and pond. For as long as I can remember, I have had a fierce curiosity and endless desire to learn. My adventures as a boy pushed me to develop an intense sense of awareness that I have carried with me throughout my life.

Between the entrance to the woods and my grandmother's house was her backyard, complete with citrus trees, palm trees, Spanish moss hanging off the canopy of the branches above, a carpet of thick Bermuda grass, a large firepit, and a chicken coop. When I was seven, my cousin and I were playing in the yard when we noticed what looked like two sandcastles in the center of her property. We approached the strange mounds and discovered they were not just made of sand. They were huge ant piles! Ants were crawling all around them.

The thriving ant metropolis in the middle of the yard fascinated us so we attempted to study insects. Using a magnifying glass we found, we took turns looking closely at the mounds as we pretended to be scientists. We collected ants from the piles, using buckets and pails, for our research. During our ant extraction, I saw they moved in consistent patterns, creating trails that led all over the yard. We spent hours following these trails before deciding which ants to collect.

All the trails brought us back to the mounds. We felt we had completed our study of the trails, so the next step of our research was learning about how ants live inside their sandy pyramids. We dove in with our hands. Bad idea. Covered in bites that stung like tiny needles we could not remove, we picked up our shovels and continued pulling out sand. The ants had established complex tunnel systems that seemed to spiral into the ground.

Obviously, we needed to dig up the mounds so we could continue our research in the soil. Shovels in hand, we got to work.

We worked diligently over the course of a few days.

We never seemed to find the end of a tunnel! My cousin and I stopped when we had dug a hole up to our knees. It was so wide that we could lie inside without being seen. The accomplishment was thrilling, and we could not wait to continue our study. As we dug out the land where the ant mounds had been, we collected ants in buckets for further inspection. We even uncovered an underground chamber filled with ant eggs and could not believe how much we were learning. As an adult, I recognize this was not the kindest way to study ants; as a child, the opportunity to learn was too compelling to walk away from.

We got home from school one day and we were devastated to find a couple men from the neighborhood filling the hole, undoing days of our labor! I ran over to them to ask what was going on. My heart sank when I learned that my grandmother had fallen into the hole as she was headed to hang up laundry to dry on her clothesline. Confused and concerned, she had called for help. The family was at work or school, but thankfully, the nearby men heard her cries and came to help her.

My adventures in the woods and my interest in the ants helped me develop my sense of awareness. In the forest, I learned to be aware of where I am and what is around me to maintain my safety. The anthill introduced me to the complex world of these tiny creatures I hadn't previously given much thought to. Those observations were magical and wondrous for my childhood self. Yet in my grandmother's backyard, I realized serious problems can occur from a lack of awareness—I had not been aware of the potential consequences of my actions. My grandmother would not have unwittingly stumbled into the hole had she known of its existence. I had no intention of putting my grandmother in that position; had I been aware of that possibility, I would have informed my grandmother of the ant research or simply not have done it.

The yard was never the same after we dug the hole. The effects of our amateur landscaping left a sandpit where grass once grew, and I did not have the awareness to foresee this. Over the next several years, I watched the ants fade away from the yard as if we had damaged their community beyond repair. Our ant experiment impacted the entire ecosystem.

Observation is a tool. We use this tool to know our *needs*, *inspiration*, and to find *understanding*. I could not develop a positive mindset before learning how I operate or what influences my choices. Through my observations of myself as well as those around me, I developed a dichotomy to help me make productive choices regardless of my circumstances, adversity I face, or feelings: *Action Versus Reaction*. I realized that with every choice we make, we are either being proactive or reactive. When we are *proactive*, we make choices based on what will yield the most productive outcome, regardless of our emotions; when we are *reactive*, we make choices based on our emotions provoked by our circumstances.

Monitor Your Emotions

Our emotions are powerful tools that become vices when we stop governing them. Before I learned to stand my ground as a child, I was subjected to regular bullying. My neighborhoods were filled with kids aching to take their aggression out somewhere, or on someone, and that someone was often me. Despite my frustration, I knew my antagonists *wanted* a reaction, and reacting would only continue the cycle of violence. I'd seen it happen countless times. There were instances when I was angry, feeling myself coming close to retaliating. However, I did not let myself *react* to my emotions. I was *proactive* and chose to smile at the face of my aggressors. This confused them and diffused the situation.

It was important I felt the emotions of anger and sadness because they let me understand what was happening to me. In this understanding, I could find acceptance that I could not control the actions of my aggressors, but I did not have to let their actions force my own. Had I let my emotions guide my choices, I could have ended up in a dangerous and bloody scuffle.

Through observation, we improve our ability to control ourselves, our thoughts, and our actions. This is essential to our personal growth. We must be proactive in our efforts to be positive; if we are not consciously choosing how to respond to a challenge, we are being reactive. Being proactive requires awareness, which cannot be achieved without observation.

As we observe our emotions, our instincts, and ourselves, we will become aware of our hobbies, habits, and routines. Hobbies are activities we do to feel inspired. Habits are settled tendencies we have that are often challenging to give up. Routines are processes and procedures we develop to manage our *needs*. Are our hobbies, habits, and routines contributing to our growth, or holding us back? Which should we let go of, and what should we introduce? We cannot make productive changes without the awareness of what already exists.

Preparation

Make a Plan for Growth

ersonal growth—the process of bettering your mental health, physical fitness, and spiritual awareness—is a journey. The first part of this journey is observation so we can evaluate the state of our minds. We learn about our shortcomings, our strengths, and what we would like to work on. Observation helps us collect the information we need to create the space we want. This information issues a strong foundation we can build upon with preparation.

Preparation is the act of creating a plan to reach our goals. I encourage planning when working toward a goal because it helps people keep their focus and avoid wasting energy on distractions. In the garden of our minds, there are two key steps to promoting new growth: clearing your space, then preparing your space.

Clear Your Space

Weeds, although important for our ecosystems, are often unwanted plants that can take over our gardens. Like the plants we want to nurture, they too need nutrients to survive. Their roots absorb nutrients from soil, but because there are only so many nutrients present, any absorbed by the weeds is less for our desired plants. Negative thoughts are like weeds; they can quickly multiply and consume the garden of our minds. Any energy we put toward negative thoughts is less we direct toward positive and productive ones. To maximize the potential of the seeds we plant, we need to remove anything that could hold them back.

Weeding is also necessary to our focus. As we prepare ourselves for personal growth, we must differentiate between our wants and our needs. Our *wants* can multiply and get out of control, while our *needs* are stable and consistent. Wants are external desires such as goods or services that are not essential to our progress or survival. Focusing on such things instead of prioritizing our needs can cost us valuable resources and energy. As we chase our desires and neglect our needs, our needs continue to increase.

After pulling out weeds so they cannot continue rooting in our soil, we need to dig into the earth to rid it of any hidden weed roots that are waiting to grow. We also want to take out any debris or decay that could prevent our future plants from growing. I call this clearing the space. Just as we clear our gardens to make room for new plants, we must clear our minds to make room for what inspires our self-motivation. We cannot find our inspiration when we are trapped by habits, hobbies, routines that steal our energy and focus.

When the soil has been weeded and cleared, it is ready to cultivate new growth. We need to choose the seeds we want to plant. We will use our understanding to pick seeds that satisfy our needs and enrich our inspiration.

Part of the preparation process is understanding the environment where we will plant our seeds. When cultivating a garden, we must consider sunlight, climate, access to water, and soil. These elements will impact the progress of our seeds. When working on ourselves, we need to prepare for balance, discipline, practice, and focus as they make all the difference in our personal growth. I worked on a class project in grade school that forever changed how I perceive the significance of preparation.

MARCUS TALES #2
Butterfly Garden Story

My fifth-grade teacher was new to my elementary school the year he taught me. He was vastly different from the older teachers at the school who'd taught generation after generation of people from my town. He introduced new and exciting activities that brought new traditions to the community. My favorite was the class Butterfly Garden, a garden designed for caterpillars and the butterflies they would metamorph into.

The thought of making such a garden thrilled the class, but our teacher warned us that the activity would require serious effort and hard work.

We went outside to look at the area around our classroom that would become our garden. My elementary school was in the woods of the countryside, surrounded by trees and filled with wildlife. Lizards, grasshoppers, and dragonflies were more common than students. Since the student population had grown too large for the small buildings, the administration set up portable classrooms. My class took place in one, so stepping outside the classroom meant walking into the great outdoors.

My teacher showed us the fifty-square-foot space between our portable and a walkway to the main building that would become our garden. It was mainly patches of grass and tiny rocks, with a few larger rocks interspersed. I remember thinking, *How will we convert this boring and ordinary space into a vibrant garden filled with butterflies?*

My teacher explained that we were to prepare the garden over the coming weeks as part of our recess activity. A few of my classmates whined with frustration that this project would limit their free play, but I could not wait to get started.

During our recesses, my teacher picked different students to rake the area, move rocks, and dig up some of the grass and unwanted debris. He ordered supplies for our project, and boxes of materials began to show up at the school—including caterpillar larvae!

Each student decorated a rock with their name that would live in our garden. By this point, the entire class was excited for the project. We began planning out the space in detail—marking where we would place different plants and choosing where various colored rocks would go. In shifts, we started to plant.

Preparing the garden required creativity, ingenuity,

and teamwork. Although we gave up our recess, we came to enjoy the process because we got to know one another better, and every day we had something to show for our work. We'd leave school proud and excited with what we accomplished each day.

A couple weeks later, all the plants had been planted, and our rocks had been placed. It was finally time—we released the caterpillars into the garden! We observed the caterpillars eat the leaves of the plants, grow, and weave silk cocoons.

We eagerly ventured into the garden every day to look for signs of change. After what felt like an eternity, we spent an entire day watching them hatch! We finally got to see the butterflies we had been craving.

When I visited my elementary school a year later, I was delighted to see butterflies still inhabited the garden. They laid eggs in this space we cultivated and the cycle of life continued.

This experience taught me the importance of preparing a space step-by-step, with careful thought and planning. While working on the garden, my classmates and I were restless and eager—we just wanted to see butterflies! However, we needed to be patient; caterpillars cocoon when they have found the right environment, and their metamorphosis cannot be rushed.

My teacher made a point to share that he knew of other schools that attempted the project and were unsuccessful. He believed our butterflies matured because of our slow and meticulous preparation. I learned that if I only chase results and ignore the process, then I risk never reaching my goals at all. Deliberate change and transformation do not come without endurance and dedication.

Preparation was essential to the success of the project. I could not force the caterpillars to become butterflies, but we created a space where they wanted to.

Observation is the first step to developing a positive mindset. With awareness, we can begin our next stage of the process: preparing for a shift in perception. This shift will come from addressing the negative habits and routines that we identified through observation.

Preparing for a shift in mindset is like choosing the seeds you will plant in your cultivated soil. Because every seed and plant will affect the ecosystem of your garden, it is vital to be deliberate and methodological in your planning. We want to foster an environment where our different seeds will flourish together. Lavender and rose are companion plants, for example, because roses attract aphids that harm the plant and lavender appeals to aphid-eating ladybugs. When planted together, lavender and rose protect each other.

As we decide which seeds we will plant in our minds, we need to address our hobbies, habits, and routines because we direct energy into all of them and they take up valuable space in our minds. If our hobbies, habits, and routines are not building up our well-being, we need to let them go and make room for new ones.

I developed a habit in the form of a thought process to help me develop a positive mindset: *Progress Versus Maintenance. Progress* is forward or onward movement toward a destination or goal, and *maintenance* is the act of addressing and fixing problems at hand. There can be no progress without maintenance, and the key is knowing the difference. Prioritizing maintenance promotes progress because problems that are ignored do not go away; they become bigger problems and take more time and energy to address than they would have early on. My hobbies, habits, and routines should be contributing to the maintenance of my well-being, therefore promoting progress in my life.

Prepare Your Space

As a gardener, preparing your space is not just important to the success of your new plants, it is key to their long-term well-being. When I was a beginner gardener, a friend gave me twenty stalks of ruellia, a plant commonly known as wild petunia. Thrilled with the bountiful present, I planted different stalks around my backyard and at the front of my house. Little did I know, this invasive species would quickly multiply, expanding and taking over my garden! When it became a nuisance, I lifted hundreds of ruellia stalks out of the ground, hoping that pulling out the roots would be the end of the problem. Unfortunately, it was rooted so deep that it continued to shoot out new stalks, yards from where I first planted it. I hadn't prepared my space for such an aggressively invasive species. To completely remove the wild petunias from my garden, I needed to dig *four* times as deep as I planted it and *five* times as wide. Its roots spread down and out farther than I could ever have imagined, leaving with me more ruellia than I could count—and a lot of laborious work to remove it.

I learned that without proper preparation, sustaining plant growth is challenging. We cannot always adapt in time to unanticipated problems, especially if we don't have the necessary resources and tools at hand. I always say to myself: "Maintenance now, for progress later." This means that the more I maintain things in their current state right now, the fewer problems I'll have in the future. If I'd researched ruellia before I brought it home, I would have learned of its invasiveness and prepared for it accordingly before I planted it. I could have pulled out the ruellia sooner, preventing it from rooting so broadly. I had ruellia growing in places I didn't anticipate and had to stop to deal with this problem before I could make progress on my other gardening goals. Preparing thoroughly and attentively always maximizes your progress.

We need to prepare our spaces for ourselves, too. Preparation is the initial step to moving into a new environment, yet we never stop preparing if we are working for continued progress. I prepare my house for the different seasons; when a frost looms, I cover my pipes to prevent them from bursting and creating a massive problem for me to deal with. In the shadow of an approaching spring, I set up air purifiers to prepare for a season of pollen so I can breathe in my house. Preparation is a form of maintenance that helps us maintain our focus and sustain growth.

3

Planting Seeds

Choose What You Will Sow

We have observed our gardens, cultivated our soil, and chosen our seeds; we have observed ourselves, prepared our minds, and decided to align ourselves with positivity. The final step of developing our positive mindset is planting the seeds of our new hobbies, habits, and routines.

Life is finicky. A sunflower is likely to grow upwards of one thousand seeds, yet only a handful will mature into plants. Seeds need the right conditions to sprout. This can be troubling for beginner gardeners because no matter how much they research and prepare, their seeds do not grow. The same can happen with new hobbies, habits, and routines. Maybe we have not figured out how to sustain our new hobbies, habits, and routines because our old ones are taking all our time and energy.

Establishing new ways of thinking and doing things is a complex process, and we may not be successful the first time around. When this happens, we return to preparing. We spend time clearing our soil so we can replant new seeds and foster their growth. This is the act of practicing. If we let our failures stop us from trying again, we will never be successful. I created a framework of thinking to stop me from falling into the trap of letting failures and mistakes stunt my growth: *Lessons Versus Barriers.*

Lessons are the results of positive thinking and deciding to face challenges as they are and seek out ways of learning from them. *Barriers* are the results of negative thinking and allowing challenges to stop us from moving forward. I avoid barriers because they hold me back and teach me nothing, and I instead seek out lessons that I can draw upon to make more informed choices in the future. When we approach our experiences with this dichotomy, we are likely to learn lessons that help us make progress rather than create barriers that hold us back. Through continuous effort and learning lessons, we can try again until we see growth.

Be Deliberate with Your Garden

We must pick our seeds carefully because they not only affect us, but they impact our communities. Our hobbies, habits, and routines include how we interact with others and how we contribute to the world. When we collectively plant seeds of love, kindness, patience, and positivity, we grow stronger as individuals and put down healthier roots as a community. These roots lead to strong and stable trees that yield fruits of success.

The more I plant seeds of love with uplifting gestures and kind words, the more I enjoy the fruits of success. To plant these seeds, I engage in meaningful conversation, look out for others, and encourage those around me to be their best selves. I believe my push to be disciplined, respectful, and caring has increased my intelligence, made me capable in my everyday actions, and inspired my ingenuity. Opportunities to grow have been abundant, with success found even in my failures; I view failure as an opportunity to learn.

Conversely, it is too easy to plant seeds of negativity in the world, which grow toxic and destructive roots. The negative seeds include bias, stereotyped thinking, and the belittling, discouraging comments we say to each other. Once they've been planted, these negative seeds germinate in our thoughts like weeds that obscure our beauty and prevent connectivity.

A community grown from toxic seeds has no cohesion, making it harder for people to sustain any connection. Miscommunication follows, which pushes people further apart. When facing obstacles without understanding, good communication, or respect, animosity and disagreement are almost inevitable. These are the kinds of disagreements that end with aggression, even violence.

We need to be conscious of what we plant because our choices affect our communities and environments. I realized this as a young boy when I worried I'd get punished for the accidental planting of a tree.

MARCUS TALES #3
Planting Acorns

As a child, I loved to practice my aim by throwing rocks, berries, and acorns at different targets. The targets could be anything from trees to fence posts to falling leaves; we children were always looking for a challenge. My cousin and I would venture all over the neighborhood looking for the best place to set up for practice.

One day, we planned to spend an afternoon throwing rocks and acorns at pails we set up in an empty lot a couple properties down from my grandmother's. We shifted our focus when I noticed something strange in an acorn I readied to throw.

It had a split down the center, revealing a sliver of orange. I called my cousin over to take a look. *What could it be?* We took turns picking at the acorn until we could pull the mysterious orange piece out. It was a kernel! I had no idea that an acorn was actually a shell encasing something else.

After realizing we could pull out the kernel, we spent the rest of the afternoon pulling kernels out of other acorns and throwing those at our targets.

My cousin and I rarely played in the same place two days in a row—we had a circuit so we would never get bored. About a month later, our circuit began again and I went to set up the pails for our throwing practice in the empty lot. Upon returning to the target I had set up the day we pulled the acorns apart, I noticed something growing out of one of the kernels—the tiny sprout of a leaf!

I couldn't believe it. I had no idea that acorns were alive. I looked up at the tree the acorns had fallen from and it dawned on me—acorns are seeds. We stopped setting up for our game and searched for other kernels that had begun to sprout. Our search demanded a keen eye and determination found only in curious children. Out of the hundreds of kernels we inspected, only a few sprouted with new growth.

As we were sorting through the array of fallen acorns, a squirrel came along, picked one from the stack we had collected, took it to a spot at the edge of my grandma's property, nibbled it, and then dug a hole and buried it in the ground.

My heart sank . . . What if the squirrel was planting a tree? Was the acorn one of the sprouted? I could get in trouble if a new tree grew out of nowhere! My cousin and I ran over to our acorn collection and smashed all of them. We were terrified of getting chastised for any rogue trees that might grow in the abandoned lot.

I now know that the squirrel could have simply been hiding the acorn as a snack for later, but at the time, I believed it to be deliberately planting the seed of a future tree. It looked like it knew what it was doing when it inspected, sniffed, and bit the acorn before dropping it in a hole and covering it with soil. I worried the lot would become a forest because of this pesky rodent.

The experience taught me that I should be deliberate with the seeds I plant because I want to control what grows where. When it comes to planting seeds in my mind, I want to be thoughtful with the hobbies, habits, and routines I develop. Without this carefulness, I could mindlessly plant seeds of hobbies, habits, and routines that are toxic to my well-being.

Every thought we have plants a seed in our minds, so we should be conscious of what we sow. I have no desire to invite harmful weeds, invasive species, or toxicity to my garden, so I do not plant seeds thoughtlessly. I choose to plant seeds of love and kindness so I am compassionate when connecting with others. Seeds of patience and positivity keep me calm and balanced in all I do, especially when confronting hardship. Growing and maintaining a garden isn't easy. Neither is maintaining a positive mindset. They can be difficult to achieve, but they are beneficial to us and our communities. The kinds of seeds we plant are up to us.

Consider Your Environment

It's important to note that not all plants can grow in all environments. Too much sun will scorch some plants, and too little will deprive others of vital nutrients. Aquatic plants won't fare well outside of water, and sunflowers will die if submerged. When cultivating a garden, we want to plant seeds that will survive the climate and other environmental factors. Similar to ourselves, we need the environment of our mind to be conducive to our hobbies, habits, and routines. Fortunately for us, our minds are far easier to change than the landscape of the earth.

If our minds are too low-light or shady for the plants we hope to grow, we need to figure out how to bring the sun to our new garden. Perhaps the branches of an old and established tree are in the way, and we need to cut them off to allow the sun to shower its rays on our burgeoning seeds. We cannot make our seeds grow everywhere; we must do what we can to support them.

Patience

Don't Rush Your Growth

Growth cannot be forced. After taking time to evaluate our space—imagine and then prepare our future garden—and plant seeds, we have to learn the next skill for our gardening journey: patience.

Our seeds are now in our soil. Maybe we see new growth peeking above the soil; maybe our seeds did not sprout and we're starting over. In either circumstance, we need to apply patience. Patience is different from the passive activity of waiting, and letting time pass until something changes. It's the act of maintaining focus and observation while waiting for something to change, and it is an active practice because it requires constant effort.

We never stop using observation as we develop new hobbies, habits, and routines, and therefore a positive mindset. Because creating new practices takes time, we cannot stop observing how they are affecting us. Neglecting to observe their progress could result in negative practices or failed attempts. Did my plant like that extra watering? Did I feel better when I decided to stretch during the day? Was I restored or exhausted after practicing a particular hobby? It's easy to crave immediate success and give up when we do not experience it. Patience reminds us that we will not bloom unless we give ourselves the time to reach that stage of our growth, and nurture that growth with regular sunlight, water, and air.

Patience can feel like agony when we are entirely focused on results and overlook the process. I spent my childhood waiting for buses with my mother, waiting for my health to improve, waiting for the bullying to stop, waiting, waiting, waiting. . . . Waiting did not come easily to me. I had to learn patience, and how to keep myself productive while working toward a far-off end. One childhood experience keeps me grounded in patience to this day as it provoked a new sense of understanding for me.

MARCUS TALES #4

Left Behind

One summer morning when I was eleven, I woke up early and jumped out of bed.

There was no way I could sleep! My uncle was taking six of my cousins and me to a theme park across town.

On a normal day, my mother left early for work, and I'd say goodbye to her from my bed. This day, she found me moving around the house. I saw her spot the clothes I'd laid on the chair by the front door. I didn't want to ruin them before it was time to leave, but I also wanted to be able to put them on quickly when my uncle arrived.

She gave me $10 so I could buy myself food at the park—I was on top of the world.

Around 6:30 a.m., my mother left the house. My uncle was to arrive two hours later, so I finished my chores, made my bed, cleaned the bathroom, and did some homework. I looked at the clock at 8:00 a.m. and could not believe that I still had to wait another thirty minutes. I double-checked my homework and went outside to bounce my basketball in my driveway to pass the time.

I went inside to check the clock. 8:05. I checked the clock again. And again. How was time moving so slowly?

8:30 at last! I looked out the window, hoping to see my uncle's car pull up to my driveway. I'd been known to be impatient, so I refrained from calling his house. I decided to wait. At 8:45, I called my grandma. She said they were running late, so he had just left and was on his way to me. I decided to get dressed in the clothes I'd set aside. To keep my mind busy, I went back outside to bounce the ball. I decided to do that for the five to ten minutes it would take them to arrive.

I *carefully* practiced drills this time, making sure to keep my clothes pristine. I practiced longer drills; I bounced the ball sideways, backward, and against the wall of my house. I did not let myself go inside to check the time. I was determined to be patient.

The sun began to shine brighter as morning shifted into daytime. I realized I was both hungry and thirsty, so I went inside to grab a snack while I waited. When I opened the door and looked at the clock, I saw it was 9:30. I called my grandmother.

"Well, baby, they left, and they should have been there," she said. As I fixed myself something to eat while I waited, I tried not to worry. I hoped nothing had happened to them. Did I go inside at the wrong time? Outside? What if I missed them? What if they called and I didn't hear it? I checked the voice mail. Nothing.

At 10:30, I figured I would be productive while I waited. I did more homework, read, did extra chores—anything I could think of to keep my mind busy.

At 2:00, I accepted that nobody was coming. I took a nap.

I woke up with a profound sadness. As I dealt with the heaviness of my emotion, I thought about the chances of getting to go to the theme park another day. I concluded that my sadness would not help me get there, so I sat down to make a list of my goals for the future. The first thing I wrote was to apologize to my uncle for whatever I did to make him leave me behind. Going to the park was number two.

A couple hours later, my uncle showed up at my house to apologize. In the chaos of getting all my cousins ready, he thought he had everybody with him. He was distracted in the car and he forgot to pick me up. He only noticed when they arrived at the park, and it was an hour of a drive too late to get me.

Anytime I find myself getting impatient, I reflect on this experience. I went through mental anguish during those hours of waiting. There were moments of fear, when I worried that something happened to my family; moments of doubt, when I questioned if I had somehow missed them; and moments of guilt, when I wondered if I'd done something to deserve it. Throughout the day, I was impatient, restlessly waiting for something to happen.

I realized none of the negative thoughts were helping

me go to the park or have a good day. It never occurred to me that I could have simply been forgotten. Had I let my negative thoughts consume me to the point that I acted upon them, and thrown a temper tantrum at my uncle or broken things in my house out of frustration, I would have prolonged my discontent and potentially created more problems for myself to deal with.

This situation may sound like a sad story, or one with an unhappy ending. Practicing patience does not guarantee we will receive the outcome we desire. What is most important about patience is that it keeps us from being *impatient*, which can result in a negative mindset that stops us from moving forward. If we stop moving forward, we stop growing.

Over the following three years, I visited the theme park eight times.

Activate Your Patience

Patience is not passive. It requires discipline and commitment. When we get excited about a new plant, we often just want it to grow faster or show signs of change immediately. This can lead us to overwater it or move it around excessively as we worry we're not doing enough to encourage it to grow. When we are eager to start a new endeavor or chapter in our lives, it's easy to want to see or feel a sense of change in ourselves. Our desire to rush the process of developing the new hobby, habit, or routine can result in a misguided assessment of our progress. But patience isn't all hard work: we can enjoy the slowed pace and admire our seeds at every stage. Whether your pomegranate seedling is freshly planted or your tree is giving you delicious fruit, take pride in the steps you make toward a goal. Patience gives us the gift of finding pleasure where we didn't expect it—and in the *becoming* of the thing we are waiting for.

In between the front of my house and my front yard is a long rectangular gardening bed. When I moved in, a four-foot-tall box hedge inside the patch soil lined the house, leaving space for some smaller plants. I considered how to use this prime plant real estate, and I had several ideas. Maybe I could fill out the space with some variegated ginger and low-lying hosta, or perhaps I could plant some coleus. During my contemplation, there was a science fair at the school I worked at. One group of students was growing different seeds with hydroponics, and among their crop were morning glory vines.

The flowers were absolutely gorgeous; royal blues blended with amethyst purples blossoming from a white center. Upon asking what the beautiful flowers were, the students were kind enough to give me some of their seeds. I brought them home, prepared the front bed, and planted the seeds.

I was so excited to see the flowers that I found myself checking the beds every day for new growth. I checked daily for two weeks, and every day I saw nothing. One day, I was delighted to see a sprout of green, only to realize it was a weed. Hastily, and slightly confused because I had spent quality time clearing the bed, I bent down and plucked it. It turned out that was not a weed at all; the first of my glories had surfaced.

Desperate to save it, I tried to replant it only to notice I had inadvertently disrupted the roots of three other seedlings near it. The roots of the four plants were intertwined, and still fragile at that stage of their growth. I did not know how wide these plants root before emerging above soil. My impatience caused me to undo two weeks of growth of four plants in one second. I couldn't believe it. I stood there in my front yard dumbstruck for several seconds, trying to come to terms with my mistake.

I am now much more conscious when I approach my seeds and seedlings, and I am patient as I wait for them to grow. I still go out to look at my plants every day, but without the pressure to see something new. Instead, I look to appreciate my plants and whatever I am fortunate to see that day.

One day, when I was still learning to be a gardener, I was looking for growth on my roses when I noticed the deep reds and purples emerging throughout the thorny green bush. Given just how many small, half-inch purple ovals were emerging, I thought this could be a significant problem. Upon closer observation, I noticed the purples were morphing into reds. As these reds looked a little like leaves, I decided to wait to worry. Over the next several days, I observed the red leaves turn green and I realized the colors signified the different stages of the plant's growth: the leaves emerged purple, matured red, and settled green. The contrasting colors were beautiful in their own right: purple and red, red and green. I learned that nature goes through stages. Had I tried to intervene and "fix" the rosebush, I would only have disrupted its natural cycle.

Patience helps us act appropriately, and only when necessary. It takes a lot of practice, and practice takes persistence.

Persistence

Don't Give Up

Persistence gives us the stamina to complete a task despite the challenges and adversity it may bring. Persistence is hard when we don't properly understand *why* we're doing something—our motivations—or what our activities *mean*—our inspirations—or the difference between the two. *Inspiration* is the internal force that drives us in meaningful directions and creates passion. *Motivation* is the external force that pushes us to act. Inspiration is unique to every person, while motivations are often shared. Both inspiration and motivation contribute to persistence—and thereby the practice of patience.

Persistence is integral to developing and maintaining positivity. We need to be persistent for our hobbies, habits, and routines to become part of our everyday life. A positive mindset should last a lifetime, so we never stop working to maintain it. Rather than let the idea of perpetual work deter us from adopting a positive mindset, we should consider the benefits of embracing challenge, continuous growth, and endless learning.

Commit Yourself to Growth

If we find ourselves becoming restless and idle, reminding ourselves to practice observation and preparation can realign our focus and thereby our priorities. If growth is our priority, we want to observe our motivations, inspirations, and their effects on our hobbies, habits, routines in order to remain on our drive toward a positive mindset.

Persistence requires dedication and consistency. As we watch our seeds grow, we have to be persistent in our care for them. We have to monitor them regularly, as well as water them and nurture their growth. Similarly, we have to be persistent in our care for ourselves. Being kind and practicing patience with ourselves while we navigate changes to our hobbies, habits, and routines is vital to the success of our positive mindset.

I enjoy propagating plants from food scraps because it's wonderful to see life continue growing from something that would otherwise end up in my compost. I propagate a carrot by cutting off the top and placing it on a jar lid filled with a bit of water. A carrot is tricky to propagate because too little water will not encourage its growth, and too much water will drown it; the water must just come up to the edge of the carrot top rather than submerge it. If the carrot top is happy, new sprouts will grow out of the top and eventually it can be planted, yielding a plant with seeds we can harvest.

Keeping the water at the optimal level for growth takes persistence as the carrot does not soak up the water at a consistent rate. Sometimes, the water I carefully pour in disappears within a day. On other occasions, I've seen a carrot top sit in the same water for a few days. Making sure the carrot top has the ideal amount of water requires consistent observation. If I forget or get too busy to check on the carrot top, it's vulnerable to dying of thirst. Without dedication on my part, the burgeoning plant could fail.

Obstacles, challenges, and hurdles will come, but

it's how we handle them that matters. Facing these difficulties with a calm mind, smile, and upbeat energy may seem challenging, but if we are persistent in our observations of ourselves and our surroundings, spend ample time planning our routines, studying our habits, and enjoying our hobbies, it's easier to maintain peace. All of a sudden, it doesn't sound impossible at all. Instead it is something we can achieve with practice and being proactive while we practice patience.

We are unlikely to improve as gardeners or positive thinkers if we are not consistent with our efforts. Persistence means we keep working so we can achieve our goals, and this became clear to me when I entered a school contest in my youth. The contest results surprised me, but I found that there are often more ways to grow than we may understand.

MARCUS TALES #5
Oration Contest

My elementary school held an oration contest at the end of my fifth-grade year. Every student was to write a speech that they would share with the class, and teachers would choose the best two to enter an all-school competition.

I'd shared countless poems and speeches at my church, so I was confident in my ability to speak. The real challenge was writing the essay and keeping it short enough for the contest's parameters. I wrote, edited, and wrote some more before practicing with my mother who gave me helpful feedback.

Our efforts were successful because I was chosen to represent my class in the all-school competition! To prepare for the contest, I shared my speech with several different congregations at church, I practiced it with the aunt and uncles who babysat me, and I said it over and over again in the shower. I had it memorized.

When it came time for the competition, my grandmother came to support me as my mother had to work. The entire school attended the assembly where the selected students would share their essays.

"Marcus Bridgewater," my teacher called me onstage. I took a deep breath, swallowed, and strode over to the podium. I made sure to smile at the crowd as I did.

"Don't you need your essay?" one of the judges asked, noticing I held no papers.

I shook my head, still smiling, and focused. I finished delivering the speech, and the audience erupted into cheers and applause! I took this to mean I had done well, and I returned to my seat feeling great. As the judges finished their deliberating, one came to find me.

"You did great, young man. You should be proud of yourself," she said.

The judges announced the two winners. They did not say my name. I heard whispers around me, in my direction: "Why didn't that kid win?" I saw my teacher look at me with shock and annoyance before he disappeared to talk to someone.

He found me afterward and explained that the judges felt one of the students could greatly benefit from the confidence boost of winning the competition and that because I had "so much going for me," I should "let him have this one." I was so confused. Sure, my academic performance was stellar, but I worked hard for that. What made me special? I didn't see what they saw. I struggled with chronic health issues, I had little access to resources, and my community was filled with violence and devastation.

It was crushing. In the car home, I tried to figure out what I could have done better. My speech must not have been good enough. My grandmother said to me, "Baby, there was nothing more you could have done. You did your best. This may happen more than we would like. Sometimes, the odds are stacked against us, but you cannot stop trying. You cannot let this stop you."

In this moment, my grandmother taught me the importance of remaining persistent in the pursuit of my goals. If I had let myself get caught up in the idea of winning, or the disappointment of losing, I would not have appreciated the growth that came from the long hours of practice and preparation. I decided to share the speech another fifteen times with different audiences in my community. With every oration, I got better. My persistence spending all that time improving as a speaker has stayed with me much longer than any elementary school award has.

I have noticed two major issues people commonly face as they try to practice persistence: persistence without observation, and persistence without dedication.

I once planted some sweet peppers underneath a holly tree, where I already had several flowers growing. I looked outside one afternoon and noticed the tree branches were shielding the peppers from the sun. I cut off the branches that were keeping the plants in the shade to help them thrive. To my delight, the peppers began to grow at a thrilling rate.

At the same time, the plants on either side of the peppers wilted until they died. They received more sunlight than they needed. It did not occur to me that cutting the branches would harm my other plants. In my drive to save one plant, I lost seven others. I was trying to be persistent in my care of the peppers, but failed to acknowledge how that persistence would affect the rest of the plant bed. I learned that persistence without observation can be detrimental, regardless of intention.

Persist with Dedication

Persistence without dedication hinders many who work toward their goals. A few years into my gardening journey, I decided to start a vegetable garden. I felt that I had learned enough to expand my garden to include fruits and vegetables. I took eleven old plastic storage containers of different sizes, drilled holes in the bottoms, filled them with soil, and placed them on a large wooden stand I built.

I bought about thirty-five young fruit and vegetable plants that all had a fair amount of root growing. I planted them in containers based on the type of plant and how much sun they needed. The project took me three times as long as I anticipated, and I used the only free weekend I had for months to do it.

A full week passed before I could check on the plants. They were doing well, and growing better than I imagined they would in such little time. However, I noticed some problems when I took a closer look. The wooden stand was killing the grass underneath it. Some of the plastic containers turned brittle after sitting out in the harsh sun and heavy rain. One container was filled with ants.

I needed to take the containers off the wooden stand so I could move it to a new patch of grass, knowing the grass would suffer and I would have to move it again. I thought it would take me half an hour to take the plastic containers off the stand so I could move it. Carrying the makeshift plant beds was laborious, and one of them broke as it was lifted up. Frustrated, I cleaned up the soil and plastic, and looked for a place to house the now homeless plants. Exhausted, I moved the stand, hauled the containers back on top of it, and sat down for a deep breath. The process took me two hours.

Two weeks later, I had time to check on the plants. They were still growing, but I faced the same problems I had weeks before: the grass was dying, two containers broke on me, and ants colonized the soil.

I tried to be persistent in my care of the plants and success of the project. Unfortunately, I did not do enough research into the effects of weather on plastic or wood on grass. The problems that developed along with my limited free time took me away from focusing on the plants as I had planned. For our persistence to pay off, we need to be dedicated.

Experiment

Take Notes and Try Again

The more that people learn of my garden and plant collection, the more questions I am asked about how to save dying plants or how beginners can get into gardening. Truth be told, I have no formal education in plant care. Everything I know, I learned from experimenting.

Experimenting educates and empowers us, as success *and* failure affords opportunities to learn. Each time I deepen my understanding of how to foster growth. I encourage all gardeners, novices and experts alike, to experiment with their plants and take notes. Experimentation helps us maintain objectivity, while encouraging us to be critical and vigilant. It also does something equally important: it reminds us to have fun. While it is true that we are observing in an experiment, we are also giving ourselves permission to try something new, to play, and to be curious.

Experimenting requires observation and analysis, which cannot be done without patience and persistence. There's no way to learn without them. The more I learn, the more I grow, and the more I can help other things grow. When learning something new becomes our goal, experimenting helps us overcome our fears of failure.

Always Learn Lessons

Once I planted purple queen, a long tubular plant that grows pink flowers, alongside various caladiums, of many different colors, in the ground. I conducted an experiment with the goal of seeing the colorful leaves of the caladiums peek over the sprawling purple tubes of the purple queen. The plants looked wonderful together until squirrels ate the roots of the caladiums. A year later, I planted layers of planter's fabric in the ground to protect the roots of my plants, only to find the caladium was not strong enough to grow through it. Today, purple queen is all that remains.

Planting caladiums and purple queen together was the first experiment. I considered it successful before the squirrels decided to feast on my hard work, so I continued with another experiment: adding the planter's fabric. This worked, but at a cost—I lost my caladiums. Nature is complex, and we cannot always account for every variable the outdoors has to offer. I now understand that not every plant can survive layers of fabric, but the same tool can keep squirrels from roots of heartier plants. Both experiments have helped me foster growth for a myriad of other plants in my garden.

Over time, a plant's roots grow deeper into the ground. After years of growing happily and healthily in the same place, a change in its environment may impact its growth, prompting a gardener to move it. Although the gardener may be reluctant and apprehensive, experimenting and taking the risk may be the only chance of saving it. In the garden of the mind, plants represent our hobbies, habits, and routines. It can be unnerving to experiment and introduce new ways of doing things, as old habits are hard to break, but it can also be what's necessary to continue our growth.

For years, I assumed I had a firm grasp of my *needs* and *inspirations*. While living at a monastery, I had the opportunity to follow the strict diet of the monks. The effects of eating limited foods, consuming certain food groups on specific days, and following a dietary schedule transformed my understanding of how to fuel my body, and thereby my mind. For example, I learned that eating breakfast provides me with energy to carry me through the day; I rarely ate in the mornings before my time at the monastery. This experiment showed me I am still learning about how my body works and how it affects my mind.

We practice our inspiration through our hobbies. During a bout of endless fatigue and darkness in college, I was introduced by a close friend to a broken piano in the prop shop he managed. I was exhausted and overworked, but I was drawn to the instrument. I decided to try fixing the piano to give myself a mental distraction. Thankfully, the damage was minor. I tinkered with the piano until I determined what the problems were, fixed them, and tuned the instrument.

Although I'd always played music when I could, having access to this piano brought me back to life. I had no idea how disconnected I had become from my inspiration, and realigning myself gave me a renewed sense of motivation. This experiment, fixing a piano so I could play music as a pastime when nothing else energized or interested me, changed the trajectory of my semester. Light filled the darkness, happiness replaced my indifference, and the sounds of everyday life harmonized into symphonies. I was fortunate that I felt compelled to fix the piano. There are times when trying something new is the last thing we want to do, but it may be exactly what we need.

The idea of experimenting may evoke imagery of white lab coats mixing together colorful chemicals until a beaker explodes into a cloud of foam and fumes. Generally, I understand experimenting to be the process of trying something new to learn what works for us and what doesn't. It can be applied to anything from gardening to mindset development, and for me personally, overcoming speech impediments.

MARCUS TALES #6
Practicing Speech

To my surprise, I've been told countless times in my adult life that people find my voice soothing; that I have masterful cadence, articulation, and tone. Until my early thirties, I thought people were making fun of me as I spent years of my childhood struggling to navigate being ridiculed and ostracized for how I sounded.

I grew up a minority in my community. I was born to a Caribbean mother and we were adopted by an American family in the Deep South. Although we looked alike in many ways, we did not sound the same at all. I naturally took after my mother when I learned to speak. The other children in my neighborhood said I sounded like a foreigner. My adoptive grandmother thought nothing of it, but her family was not as kind.

On top of my unique accent, I also dealt with a speech impediment. My lisp and rhotacism provided more ammunition for people to use against me. I was never around anyone who sounded like me. At school, I was made fun of for having a lazy tongue and slurring my *R*s; at church, the children teased me for sounding foreign; when four of my cousins moved in with my grandmother, I was no longer safe at home. I could never let my guard down.

I began attending a speech therapy class at school when I was five. I had to practice saying my *R*s and *S*s; if I was successful in my pronunciation, I got to pick a prize from my teacher's treasure chest. She was a special teacher who only came in every so often to help students like myself. I admired her patience, and the way she responded to mistakes with kindness. She never held mine against me, which made me comfortable and open to genuinely practicing. No matter how much I struggled, muscles aching, eyes filling with frustrated tears, she encouraged me to continue.

My impediment and the teasing it brought lasted for another several years. During the break between semesters of my third-grade year, I started writing more. I needed to find a way to deal with the nervousness I felt at every moment, and writing became my escape. Writing gave me confidence. When my third-grade teacher asked if anybody wanted to share their story from a class activity aloud with the class, I volunteered. I figured I would embrace my anxiety and take the opportunity to practice speaking.

Practicing in class helped, but it was not enough. So I continued to experiment. I began reading my journal entries aloud to myself. When I heard sounds on the radio or the television, I tried to mimic them as best I could to the point that my jaw and tongue were sore for a full day. I'd speak less until my muscles relaxed and I could resume my practice. I was committed to mastering my voice. By fourth grade, my speech teacher told me I had improved enough to no longer need classes. I felt strange; I had been working with my speech teacher for years at this point and she was one of the few people in my life who had been consistently kind to me.

I did not feel like I deserved to leave the class. Yes, I had improved significantly, but I felt like I still had a long way to go. For the next few years, I kept experimenting. I took every opportunity to try something new in order to perfect my pronunciation.

To this day, I still find myself surprised that I can speak the way I do. Nobody would guess how many hours I spent as a child learning to contort my face, strain my muscles, and make different sounds so I could speak without the impediments. My speech experimentation took years, but I was determined to learn from every practice and continue improving.

Never Stop Learning

Taking notes helps us document the progress of our experiments. When it comes to myself, I always fall back on journaling. It's one of my favorite ways to take notes, and a helpful tool for self-reflection. It helps me analyze my *needs*, *inspirations*, and *understanding*, as well as helps me track my progress with my developing hobbies, habits, and routines. The more notes I take on what works and what does not work, the more information I have to guide my choices and experiments in the future.

Journaling should be a no-pressure activity that

helps us learn about ourselves. I often use a prompt to lead my writing when I am focused specifically on personal growth. I create two columns: I title one of them *What I Am Doing*, and the other *What Am I Feeling?/What Do I Notice?* I might write under the *Doing* category, *I woke up and stretched.* The corresponding *Feeling/Noticing* column entry would read, *Stretching eased my tight muscles and improved my mobility. I felt energized and ready to start my day.*

After several days of taking notes, I go back to review what I have written. I look for patterns, changes, or anything that can tell me about myself. Perhaps I did not stretch one morning and wrote about how sore and stiff I felt that day—this would teach me that stretching plays an important role in my morning routine.

Ultimately, experimentation is a way to improve self-motivation. If you have decided to learn from your experiences to fuel your personal growth, experimenting is a great tool. It allows you to build on the information you gather and try new things without a fear of failure, as even failure provides lessons. Every seed we plant is an experiment, as well as the different ways we try nurturing their growth. Our hobbies, habits, and routines are attempts to satisfy our *needs*, enrich our *inspiration*, and harness our *understanding*. Some of these attempts will move us forward, directly toward our goals. Others will redirect us until we find a new path. Our best shot at success comes from patience, persistence, and practice—and reminding ourselves that we cannot force our growth, only foster it.

In Sum

I began working on my positive mindset long before I started gardening, but caring for my plants reinforced everything I knew about the process. I had to observe my space to learn about its features and how I could turn it into a garden, just as I had to observe myself to learn about what I could do to support my own growth. Preparation follows observation, because change cannot be rushed or forced. Developing new hobbies, habits, and routines takes time—they are not established overnight and are best achieved when we are in the nurturing environment they need. I must be patient and persistent in my care for my plants, because they may need my help as they bloom and mature. If I fail, I practice, and try again. Growth comes in many forms. What works for one plant might not work for another, so I experiment, and encourage myself to try new things and keep learning.

Once our seeds have rooted and begun to reach for

the sun, unfurl their leaves, and bloom their flowers, we know that we have achieved the first step of our journey toward a positive mindset. To sustain the growth of our plants, we must continue observing their progress, monitoring their soil, and maintaining their health. Neglecting to water them, rid them of infestations, or protect them from harsh weather could destroy all our hard work.

We cannot give up on our new hobbies, habits, and routines once they've become part of our everyday life; we must maintain them so we can appreciate their benefits over time. Growth is a continuous process and without reason to stop, it won't. It may evolve and take on new forms, but it will remain consistent in its objective—keep growing.

Our minds are gardens, and they can be beautiful, vibrant, and full of life. With dedication and a willingness to nurture, our plants can grow.

Learning from Trees, Practicing Observation, and Taking Notes

In this activity, we'll practice our skills of observation and taking notes to monitor our growth.

1. Acquire a journal and writing utensil. Write down the date and time.

2. Head to your backyard, local park, or anywhere you can closely observe a tree.

3. Stand about ten feet away from the tree or far enough that allows you to see most of it. If it's a very tall tree, don't worry if you cannot see the top of it.

4. Take a moment to appreciate the roots, trunk, branches, and other qualities such as leaves, flowers, or fruit.

5. Imagine that every branch you see has roots to support it growing beneath the ground.

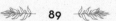

6. Consider its age, how it's withstood the seasons, and how it's adapted to continue growing.

7. Recognize that you are like this tree: a living being that has endured, triumphed, and continued growing despite any obstacles. Use this experience as an opportunity to reflect on what you've been through, where you are, and what you can do to support your growth.

8. Write down your observations, conclusions, and how the experience makes you feel. Let your *inspiration* guide your writing.

Note: Journaling is a powerful tool I use to log my experiences, emotions, and reflections. I have many journals filled with entries structured like this activity. They've become some of my most valuable assets, providing resources I can use to understand and appreciate my progress, as well as to identify if I need to make changes to my hobbies, habits, and routines. Our growth, like that of a tree, is incremental and can be hard to notice or appreciate if we don't stop to observe it. We can use journals to reflect on how much we've grown and make sure we are still on the track of growth we desire.

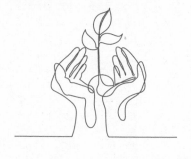

PART TWO

Physical Fitness

Managing Growth

f you were a plant, what would you be?

A leafy palm, a spiky air plant, or a shiny watermelon peperomia?

Regardless of the height of your stem or the size of your leaves, you must learn the hobbies, habits, and routines you need to grow. Different plants, even variations of the same species, frequently need distinct care. Tending to my first dieffenbachias made this clear to me.

I bought three: silver, white, and variegated. Beautiful plants with radiant colors and large, soft, oval-shaped leaves, they were a delight to add to my collection. After bringing them home, the vibrance of their leaves unfortunately began to fade, replaced by yellowing and browning on the edges. Was this a sign of normal growth or was it a problem? The silver showed the worst signs of decay with more than two-thirds of the plant in decline.

I began to look closely at the plants, noticing that parts of the leaves had become misshapen and the stocks were starting to lose their form. I reached down to touch them and noticed the consistency in their structure had gone from firm to mushy.

I had been watering all three the same but they weren't thriving the way I had hoped, and I was forced to realize: although they were very similar plants, their stages of maturity were different as well as their growth patterns. I could not care for each plant with the same routine—I had to give each plant individual care. This reflects how we, as people, must care for ourselves.

Setting up a lush and lively garden takes thoughtful planning, and this parallels how I nurture my mental health with a positive mindset. Tending to each plant individually, knowing they all need specific care, reflects how I care for my body. Just as every plant needs varying amounts of water and sunlight, physical fitness looks different for everybody.

We often think of peace when we define mental well-being, so what defines physical well-being? For me, the answer is balance. Much like peace is a state of mental calm and clarity, balance is a state of physical control and stability. So how do we achieve this?

Maintaining the connection between the mind and body sustains our peace and balance. The more we nurture the connection between mental health and physical fitness, the stronger the mind and body become. When the connections are ignored, our energy is wasted; when they are neglected, our energy is diminished. The body is a collection of parts that come together to work as one, and every part is fueled by the same energy source. For this reason, energy management is essential to maintaining a healthy well-being. How we use our energy is more than what we eat to fuel ourselves, it's also how we think about our bodies and what we decide to prioritize.

We often associate physical fitness with athletes or people in gyms whose muscles bulge out of their shirts as they raise hundreds of pounds above their heads, faces contorted with concentration as they sweat heavily. We think of competitions and complex diets. We're presented with ideals of what optimal physical fitness looks like as if we don't range in size and shape. Yet I see physical well-being in a different way.

Let's think of ourselves as plants as we work on our physical fitness. With a growth-focused mindset, we direct our energy toward improving our understanding of our physical well-being. I suggest five core components to our physical well-being. First, pay attention to what energizes us. Where does our sunlight come from? Second, recognize when we are in health and when we are in stress. We all wilt at times: knowing the signs of problems helps us address them and get our leaves to perk up. Third, appreciate ourselves more. We truly begin to blossom as we relinquish judgment of ourselves and embrace the colors, shapes, and textures that make us who we are. There is no need to compare ourselves to others when we respect our own qualities. Let's learn to let go of any judgment we have and remember a rose is no better than a tulip; each has its own charm and purpose. Fourth, pay attention to physical stimulation and how it makes us feel. Plants respond to stimuli (light, water, soil) in a multitude of ways. Let's consider our own responses to stimuli, like our reactions to pleasing textures or cold weather. Fifth, design a new outlook toward our physical fitness, one rooted in healing. Our bodies are layered. Let's expand our understanding of ourselves so we can easily identify such problems and find restorative practices to remedy them.

Because every person is unique in their body, I don't see physical fitness as something we can universally prescribe. I look at the different shapes, colors, and textures of the plants in my garden and smile at the intricate scene I see. As much as I love plants, my garden would not compel me the same way if I only had one species growing in it. The diversity creates a layered aesthetic with something to appreciate at every angle. Every plant brings something special and contributes to the overall wonder that is my space, and I help them prosper by paying attention to their specific needs. I can't help but admire the gorgeous space I have designed.

I imagine that my plants must be in a state of peace as they are always trying to grow. Regardless of the adversity they face—harsh weather, broken stalks, chewed roots, stifling location—as long as they are still alive, they are working to maintain balance. They will continue trying to push out new stems, leaves, and roots and grow. Let's learn to do the same.

PHYSICAL METAPHOR

Neglecting Your Garden

After carving your path from the desert through the thick dense brush, you find a community of others who made the same journey. They invite you to join their community as long as you are willing to work when you are called upon.

You're taken to an enchanting garden filled with beautiful greenery and exotic foliage. Vines hang from an overhead trellis, and garden beds of varying shapes and sizes are homes to collections of plants radiating health. Flowers of every color imaginable surround you. In the center of the garden is a rosebush, deep red petals glistening with dew amid the prickly thorns. After exploring the wonders of this oasis, you're given keys and told it's yours to care for.

The first few years of watching over the garden are delightful. You marvel in the ways the plants respond to your care. You spend time tending to the plants day in and day out. There are colors, shapes, and textures of all kinds for you to explore. After years of enriching enjoyment, you're told the garden must produce a certain number of flowers and fruit, which will be sold. This new pressure changes how you perceive your time in the garden—suddenly, you're on a schedule. You stop walking around the entire garden and nurturing every plant to focus on what you can encourage to produce. You turn off your curiosity, and along with it your gratitude for the diversity.

You shift your focus to the plants that can produce what can be sold.

The vines, desperately thirsty for water, shrivel on the trellis and fall to the ground in brittle pieces of gray.

Mites go unnoticed in a neglected bed of caladiums. They feast on the nutritious plants, multiply, and claim the other beds as their own. The foliage slowly decays, withering into shades of brown. In your stressed frenzy, you find yourself spending more time with the reliable rosebush that gives you enough flowers to satisfy your quota.

One day, someone stops by. You open the door and exchange quick courtesies before you say, "I can't talk right now, I'm working in my garden." The person looks defeated as you close the door.

Time passes . . .

The debris makes your passage through the garden harder. Between the piles of dead plants you need to step over and the remnants of foliage you need to dodge and duck under, it takes you twice as long to reach the rosebush as it initially had, and twice as long to care for it. You notice the roses have gotten smaller, and so has your yield. A glimpse of your face in a puddle shows you your skin has paled and dark circles developed around your eyes. You find yourself deflated, unsettled, and uninspired.

It had not always been this way. You'd once enjoyed this space and the life that thrived within it. What happened to the vines that used to tickle your face as you made your rounds? You attempt to look up above you to see the vines. A painful stiffness stops you. Your back cannot straighten enough for you to angle your head to the trellis as you've spent years bent over the rosebush. For the first time you begin to notice how sore you feel.

When you inspect the rosebush, it's clear that the dregs of the garden have piled onto the soil of the rosebush, inviting infection and infestation. You've not only let the garden fall apart, but your final crop has started to fail you.

The perceived pressure to meet the quota skewed your approach to the garden. Surveying the decrepit garden makes you realize you could have managed the garden differently. The garden was an assortment of different plants that created an ecosystem of symbiosis; as soon as one plant bed died, the others followed suit. The same is true for you. You let yourself go without maintenance, and now your skin, back, and body are failing you.

We live in a fast-paced society that values efficiency and output. The timelines of production do not always allow us time to tend to our well-being the way we need to in order to keep up. Settling into a routine of hunching over the rosebush makes it challenging to retrain our muscles to support our bodies to stand up straight. If we neglect the entirety of the garden to focus on one plant, there is no guarantee the flowers, vines, and foliage will return to their full health. Failing to address the infestation and onset of mold that grows among the fallen garden will ultimately catch up with you when the rosebush meets its peril.

We can avoid becoming the gardener and the rosebush by staying focused, paying attention, and listening to our bodies. We can think critically about how we use our energy, look for signs of illness and injury, evaluate the layers of ourselves, and seek out ways to heal. Check in with yourself, and prioritize your well-being. We should marvel at the beauty of our bodies rather than simply value them for appearance or efficiency. And we must understand that physical wellness requires an understanding of all levels of need, from rest to nourishment to self-acceptance.

Energy

Establish Rhythm and Find Balance

Every moment of every day, the plants in my garden absorb oxygen, air, and sunlight and harness their power to grow. New leaves sprout when old ones fall, and these nourish the soil as they decompose. The plants soak up these nutrients with their roots, and the cycle continues. Nothing is wasted, and energy flows continuously between plant and soil. The same can apply to our human bodies.

Paying attention to what energizes us is the first core component of physical well-being because how we use our energy determines whether or not we can maintain our balance. There is a constant exchange of energy in the universe. This constant movement creates rhythms that all flow together. Just as the sun rises and sets every day, and the ocean tide moves higher up the coastline before retreating, our hearts are always pumping blood in and out, creating a beat. Life exists in a perpetual state of ebb and flow, following a natural rhythm that keeps it balanced. We too move to rhythms; our body has an internal rhythm, our heartbeat, and an external rhythm, our breath. These two rhythms should work together.

It's always fascinated me how our hearts begin to beat and establish a rhythm long before we take our first breath of air. This rhythm sustains us for the rest of our lives and is supported by our breath. The breaths we take energize our bodies with every beat of our hearts. We can control our heartbeat with our breathing and establish healthy rhythms that support our peace and balance.

Our hobbies and habits create routines that affect our rhythms because they direct our energy. Understanding the effects of our hobbies, habits, and routines helps us maximize our energy and sustain it for as long as possible. When we don't make time to reflect and do maintenance to our rhythms, we get off tempo. This is a problem because it can slow us down and push us away from growth.

We can apply our awareness to evaluating our energy, and check in with our hobbies, habits, and routines. When did you wake up, and how did you sleep? Are you hungry? When and how do you move as the day progresses? Where, how, and when did you get energy? What are you doing to care for yourself, from brushing your teeth to stretching? Then ask yourself, *Are my hobbies, habits, and routines helping me grow?*

To answer these questions, check in with your needs. Are you a full-sun plant, or partial shade? Are you a succulent that needs monthly watering, or a coleus in the summer heat that needs near-daily hydration? As a person, how many meals do you need to eat a day? How many hours of sleep do you need to feel refreshed and alert? Your *needs* should influence your hobbies, habits, and routines to support your rhythms and keep you balanced.

Pace Yourself

Pause for a moment, and smell the air. What does it smell like? Now, take a deep breath. Does the air smell the same? Was the breath you took to smell any different from the deep breath? What is your heart rate? We don't always think about our heartbeats or how we breathe, or how they are connected—they're just happening in the background. When our most basic rhythms become background noise, we may find ourselves easily fatigued or shoved off balance. The more off balance we are, the harder it is to get back to center. Balance begins with breathing because it keeps energy moving through our bodies and sets a pace for how we use our energy.

Learning to manage my energy showed me how important it is for maintaining momentum. I had to learn to pace myself as I had a tendency to push myself to the point of exhaustion at different points in my life. I'd overwork my roots, have to wait while they healed, and lose valuable time in the process. Once I harnessed the relationship between my breath and my heartbeat, I could pace myself and avoid running out of energy. Because we can breathe absentmindedly, it may seem like some insignificant part of our physiological workings. Yet we are breathing *all the time*. Control of our breath brings more control over ourselves, so we should consider how our breath affects our rhythm. I suggest incorporating breathing exercises into our routines.

If I notice something is threatening my balance, I do this breathing practice: Breathe *in* for three seconds, *hold* for five seconds, and breathe *out* for six seconds. I'll do it once, or repeat it twice more, taking a couple minutes' break between the three reps. It steadies me, improves my air circulation, and helps me find clarity.

Global news, social media, the pressure to move quickly, and other everyday stressors can be adversaries to our steady rhythms. We are often unaware of the effect on our breath, and thereby our heartbeat, when we react to information we read online, rush to answer an email, or sit in traffic. These situations tend to put pressure on our mind, taking us away from our peace and positive mindset.

With the mind's effect on the body, losing our peace can put us off balance, making it harder for us to find a healthy rhythm again. To review, the mind is balanced by *needs*, *inspiration*, and *understanding*; needs are of the body. If the body's needs are disregarded, our positive mindset is compromised.

As our hobbies and habits become routines, we settle into our patterns and our routines become mindless. It can become harder to notice if our routines are neglecting our well-being or our environment, so it is important that we check in with ourselves and our routines frequently. I learned this when my mom and I moved into our first house and I discovered my chore routine was not as thorough as I thought it was.

MARCUS TALES #7
Our First House

I spent most of my childhood sharing rooms, sleeping on floors, and living in small spaces. When I was nine, my mother told me she had a surprise for me. We were going to get a house! I was in absolute disbelief.

I could barely process the idea of having a house to ourselves. We'd spent the past seven years with my adoptive grandmother in her one-story two-bed/one-bath house. It didn't feel like too small of a space until my four cousins joined us three years in. I'd been grateful to simply have walls and a roof; in retrospect, seven people sharing one bathroom was a daily challenge. Once we moved into our new place, I found there was a lot more work involved in caring for a house than I realized. The extra space brought me more responsibility.

"The house will only last as long as we keep it," my mother would say. In response, I developed a routine of chores. My housework included sweeping leaves and dirt off the porch, washing pollen and dust off the windows, and cutting the grass. As I immersed myself in the new responsibilities of homeownership, I thought of how similar caring for a house is to caring for our bodies.

The grass on our lawn was always growing, so I needed to trim it regularly to keep it neat; if I don't tend to my hair regularly, it will become disheveled and unkempt. I bathe routinely to keep myself clean the same way I washed the windows at our house. Neither of us will stop collecting particulates and amassing dirt.

Months passed, and I decided to reexamine the house. I typically entered and exited the house through the roll-up door in our attached garage. For the first time since moving in, I decided to exit the house through the side door at the back of our garage. This door, which opened to the side of the house in between the front lawn and backyard, was much harder to open than I remembered. Upon closer inspection, I realized it was stuck.

I unlocked the door, exited the house through our front door, and pushed against the garage door with all my might until I managed to get it open. I took a moment to look closely at the door frame. It had weathered shut, and its hinges were sealed with debris. This layer of grime would have worn away had we used the door more frequently. The door wasn't the only problem: ants had begun collecting in a corner behind some storage containers and gone unnoticed as we were not in the garage often enough to see them.

After spending an afternoon trying my best to fix the door, I thought about my chore routine. My mother, terrified of snakes and lizards, had avoided the garage as much as she could since we had moved in. Meanwhile, I'd gotten into a rhythm of working all over the house but didn't realize the garage door needed to be included in my routine. It dawned on me: I'd been caring for something, but only part of it.

I had settled into a rhythm when I thought my routine was helping me accomplish my goal of keeping the house in order. Yet settling stopped me from noticing that my routine was incomplete. If I had not reexamined the house, the door would have become harder to open and the ant infestation would have worsened. Stopping to reevaluate what I was doing allowed me to see what I had missed so I could improve my routine and fall into a better rhythm.

Once we find our rhythm, our main task is keeping pace with it. Our physical well-being is dependent on it, just like a house. What is your broken door? What hasn't been attended to lately? Another way to explore this is by asking yourself regular tune-up questions: Am I tired, and if so how can I recharge? Am I unwell, and if so what is the right remedy for me? One of the most important questions we can ask ourselves is, am I growing? Am I thriving? Sometimes, we may think we are doing "good enough" when we could be doing better. Ask yourself, am I using my energy in the right way? I think often of a dying neon sweet potato ivy I bought from the discount section of the plant store. It caught my eye because I noticed new growth in the center of the pot. It appeared to have been encouraged to grow out rapidly, possibly from too much fertilizer, but not enough time in between doses. I took it home, determined to nurse it back to health. I trimmed it back, cut off as many dead leaves as I could, and watered the soil a little bit.

Within weeks, the tiny leaf that I'd noticed in the store grew into a mature plant that shot out more and more leaves. My suspicion had been right: the plant was expending too much energy on the dying stems and leaves, and it had a better chance at surviving if it could redirect its energy into the new growth. This reminded me that how we use our energy matters. Knowing how we use it prevents us from wasting it and stunting our growth.

Colors

Strive for Balance

U sing colors to evaluate our bodies is the second core component of physical fitness. In my understanding of physical well-being, I consider colors as a way to gauge how healthy something is, whether that is a plant in my garden or my own body. This is because colors create patterns, and if a pattern has an inconsistency, there might be a larger problem. In a bush of pink roses, a flower with brown petals stands out, which could be a sign that the bush is malnourished and unable to provide nutrients throughout the plant. A yellowing leaf on a green pothos vine can mean the plant has been overwatered or is suffering from an infestation. A purple shade on my skin can be a sign that I bruised a muscle.

Learning to see color objectively means making assessments, not snap judgments. We don't want to look at a yellow leaf and immediately assume we know why it faded from a vibrant green—we need to be patient and thorough as we search for the cause of the problem. If I treated a plant for an infestation when it only needed less water, I could cause more damage to the plant and create more issues for myself to deal with. The same is true with our bodies. Nothing in nature is arbitrary—every color has a purpose. To stay balanced and manage our physical well-being, we need to look for understanding in what we see.

Observe Color, Find Patterns, and Know When Our Bodies Are Unwell

Colors can indicate the state of our body. A good meal, quality sleep, and lack of stress gives us a healthy glow. Exhaustion brings dark pigmentation under our eyes, while stress and sleep deprivation leave us looking pale. I observe this in people around me as regularly as I do in my garden: When my plants have sufficient water, nutrients, and sunlight, they look strong, full, and vibrant. I can tell when something is off because their petals, leaves, and vines are muted or inconsistent in their colors.

Everything in nature is constantly changing, and we can see signs of these changes in color. The key is knowing the difference between normal color changes and sickness or injury.

There are hundreds of types of philodendrons, a viny plant known to climb up trees. Each has distinct color patterns. With practice, we can see variance in color, enabling us to see subtle differences in the species. The heart-shaped leaves of the Brasil philodendron are distinguished by dark green leaves with tails of yellow trailing down the center. After learning its color pattern, it's easy for me to identify this plant among other philodendrons, as well as identify when a philodendron is sick, such as browning leaves from sun damage.

Like the Brasil philodendron, all living things have color patterns that reveal when they are in health or under stress. When I worked as a teacher, I applied this to my observation of my students every day. I knew what they looked like when they were balanced—getting sleep, eating enough, playing outside—and I could tell when someone was unwell and unbalanced because the color of their face, hands, or eyes would change.

I would ask, "How much sleep did you get last night?"

They'd say, "How did you know I didn't get much sleep?"

Upon asking how they used their time, I found that, on top of their homework and extracurriculars, they were often spending hours on the internet instead of sleeping. I'd encourage them to prioritize rest, address their routines so they could better manage their energy, and return to a balanced state.

It is important to note that our bodies can become unbalanced for reasons outside of our hobbies, habits, and routines. We may experience injury, illness, and chronic pain for reasons we cannot control. Developing new habits and routines may help treat our ailments but may not serve as cures. I cannot change the weather or the will of the animals and insects who engage with my plants; I can only monitor my garden and address the issues I see. When we experience chronic pain or illness, we can do one thing that is similar to a gardener observing the colors of his plants: pay attention. We should observe our bodies so we can best use our energy in whatever state we are in, whether that means an ice pack on a chronic back problem or a cup of water with lemon for a regularly upset stomach. Even if we cannot cure, we can still be gentle and attentive to our physical needs.

What are your colors telling you? Do you need to be watered, repotted, or moved to a new location? Is the sun getting brighter with changing seasons, and burning your leaves?

I learned the importance of paying attention through an injury I experienced as a young man. I tried to ignore the injury as long as I could, but the color changes on my skin made it clear that I had a problem. It took weeks for me to heal and return to a balanced state, but it showed me that the colors of our bodies should not be overlooked.

MARCUS TALES #8
The Broken Collarbone

I made sure to sit as close to the front of the bus as I could so I could be the first one of my friend group to get off the bus at our neighborhood stop. Our week-long game of tag had been intense; we'd waited for each other in school bathrooms, outside of each other's classes, anywhere we could to tag someone else. Eager to tag someone else, I was currently "it."

After getting off, I walked around the bus and waited to tag my friend where he wouldn't see him. As I stood there, feeling the weight of my heavy backpack dig into my shoulders, I realized I wanted to talk to my friend instead of play the game. I watched him walk down the steps of the bus, notice me, and immediately put some distance between us, him anticipating my next move.

"Let's call a truce until tomorrow," I yelled to my friend. He grinned at me, which I took to be an acceptance of the truce. I started running down the hill of the neighborhood to catch up with him. Thinking I'd begun to chase him, he dropped his backpack from his shoulders and sprinted away from me.

I was too close to his backpack to avoid it and tripped over it as I fell down the hill. My backpack, heavy with my thick textbooks, rolled with me, falling onto my head, neck, and shoulder as I rolled over twice. In a state of shock, I hopped up off the ground and looked around.

All the kids from the neighborhood stopped what they were doing and looked at me with huge eyes. My friend approached me and asked, "Are you okay?"

"I called truce!" I responded. He hadn't heard me and believed I'd started running to tag him.

"Are you okay?" he repeated. "That was a heck of a fall."

I wasn't sure if I was okay, but I was determined to be. The last thing my mother needed was something new to deal with, especially when she came home late at night after a long day of work. The left side of my body throbbed. Trying to ignore it, I picked up my backpack, wincing as I pulled on the straps, and walked home hoping to nurse it myself before my mother came home. Like I did with most injuries.

"You don't look so good," my friend said to me warily as I waved to him and walked toward my house.

I made it through the door and let out a sigh of relief when I took off my backpack. Exhausted, I thought eating something would help me get my energy back so I could feel better. I made a snack and sat on the couch in front of my TV, only to see that a crossover episode of my favorite shows, *Power Rangers* and *Teenage Mutant Ninja Turtles*, was on! But the throbbing was growing unbearable, and I frustratingly couldn't concentrate on this once-in-a-lifetime television crossover spectacular.

Food didn't help, and the pain was impossible to ignore. I reluctantly pulled aside my shirt at the collar to examine my shoulder, which was black, blue, red, and undeniably swollen. Food and relaxing hadn't eased the pain, so I thought I'd try a bath. I ran one and got in the water with all my clothes on. Unbeknownst to me, I was experiencing delirium, and it was becoming harder for me to think with every minute.

The warm water did nothing for the throbbing.

Colors

Another inspection of my shoulder showed me the colors had deepened. I realized I'd need to remove my shirt so I could see the area in full, but I couldn't lift my shoulder so there was no way I could pull off my T-shirt. My only option was to cut the shirt off, which I did unwillingly because I didn't want to ruin a nice shirt.

By this point, my right hand tingled and had started to lose color. I cut the shirt diagonally from the bottom left to the right shoulder so I could look at the area. I'd done my best to feel better and ignore the pain, but seeing the severe discoloration forced me to recognize that something was wrong. I couldn't fix it on my own. Defeated, I called my grandmother.

She came over immediately but before she could say anything, I asked, "Do we have to tell my mother?"

"Let me see," she replied. After a quick glance, she looked at me and said, "Yes we do. We have to go to the hospital."

Several hours and a couple x-rays later, the doctors informed us that I'd broken my collarbone when my backpack landed on me after I tripped. Coincidentally, my mother worked at the nursing home behind the hospital and was able to meet us quickly. She wasn't angry, or at least she didn't show it, and understood I didn't break it out of reckless behavior or goofing off. They stayed with me till it was time to go home.

This experience taught me that when the body experiences physical trauma, it can be seen through colors. Discoloration is a signal that the body is using energy differently. Even if we don't know what the discoloration means, stopping to pay attention to the signal helps us keep our balance. One part of the body could be expending energy in a way that draws from the others, putting a strain on the body as a whole.

As time passed, my body healed and the color of my shoulder area returned to my normal skin color. Each change in hue matched an increase in my strength and mobility. When my body was fully healed, there were no signs of an inconsistency in the color pattern of my skin.

Stages in Color, Stages in Life

Color in our bodies can indicate health, but it ultimately points to *growth*. When a plant has a bright green tip at the ends of its branches, it is a clear sign that it is expanding and growing.

The stalk of my trumpet plant is an olive brown with a rough texture resembling that of a tree branch. It tends to grow upward with height, producing a new stem of a smooth youthful green that will inevitably deepen over time to match its mother stalk. I know the plant is alive and healthy when I see a new sprout of green every spring. It blooms delicate pink flowers until winter when its parakeet green leaves fade to dull yellow and fall off, leaving a leafless olive-brown stalk before spring approaches once more.

Our bodies go through stages throughout our lifetime. They are in a constant state of motion and change, always preparing for the next chapter. Color, therefore, not only signals potential harm, illness, or injury, it also shows us growth and maturity. The colors of our bodies will change over time, just like those of the trumpet plant. Remember that aging *is* growing, even though we don't typically describe it in this way.

The changes in the trumpet plant's colors are part of how it grows and thus part of its life's cycle. It means it's healthy and able to support itself. People are quick to feel sad, shamed, or distressed at the first sighting of a gray hair. While there's nothing wrong with mourning the end of one stage of our lives, there's no need to dread or deny what's to come. Let's celebrate our growth the way I do when I see a hint of green growing among the olive brown, even when that growth is a gray hair. A lack of change would signify a lack of growth.

The process of growth is incomplete without every stage. My peppermint hibiscus plant blooms the most beautiful pink and white flowers the sizes of saucers. I'm fortunate if I can admire them on summer mornings because they wilt by the afternoon and fall off the plant come sundown. Over the course of the following days, the fallen flowers fade to brown as they decay, and new flowers bloom at sunrise.

This process reminds me of the cycle of life: The hibiscus cannot keep flowering without old blooms falling and making room for new growth. From the green of a new stem to the vibrant blooms to the brown of the fallen petals, every color marks the beginning and end of another stage in the plant's progress. Newborns often have a purple or red tint to their skin that fades to the baby's skin tone in time. The colors of our bodies change as we bloom from children to adults, signifying we are ready to foster growth in new ways. With each year that passes, we continue changing. Our skin may darken or lighten, age spots appear—even the colors of our lips fade.

Like my hibiscus, we grow through stages for a reason. We have to support and nurture the growth of our first set of leaves so they can collect sunlight and create energy for our flowers. After we finish blooming, we prepare the next generation of flowers for success with the nutrients our petals give to the soil. This process takes time and can only be done in stages. To fully support this growth, we have to appreciate each stage. Respect every stage of the process; there is balance in the arc of life.

Shapes

Appreciate Form

The third core component of physical fitness is embracing the shape of our body and all its parts. Like plants, we vary immensely in shape, size, height, and width. In a world where we are constantly presented with examples of ideals, be it a physique or a facial structure, we can forget health and beauty do not take any one shape—they look different for everybody.

One of my favorite plants, epiphyllum, commonly known as curly locks, is a type of hanging cactus. Its unique characteristic is its fat curly stems that grow in spiraling tendrils. I've never seen another plant that shares its shape.

My first epiphyllum was among the original sixteen plants I was given that sparked my interest in gardening. It was also among the bunch that I managed to keep alive and propagate. I propagated it as much as I could and put it all over my garden because I found it so exquisite.

I was shocked when several friends and neighbors commented on how displeasing it was to look at. They didn't like its shape; everything I appreciated about the plant was off-putting to them. A little saddened, I knew I couldn't force anyone else to like the plant as beauty is in the eye of the beholder. I realized I can't change what others think is pleasing, and I don't need to change what I think is beautiful. Ideals of beauty aside, its uniqueness made it stand out. Everybody who saw it commented on it, both positively and negatively.

Plants are diverse. In one sweeping glance at my garden, I see a landscape of varying shades of green punctuated by pink roses, the white leaves of a spider plant, yellow and brown leaves collecting in my plant beds, and the purple flowers of my ruellia. Everywhere I look is an assortment of shapes, colors, and sizes of plants that I can appreciate.

This reminds me of us as human beings, our bodies, and the diversity we represent. If we think of ourselves as plants, we can begin to see these varying body shapes without judgment. Think instead about what to celebrate, from large strong thighs built from hard work to a mole that makes a face unique. Every one of my plants has its color, shape, and size, and each contributes to the beauty of my garden. There are reasons for the differences among plants, and each is a gift. I think of my cactus that has smaller leaves than other plants to prevent losing water in the arid summer heat. In contrast, the broad leaves of my elephant ears are perfect for catching rain water and funneling it down to the soil for its roots to soak up when temperatures cool. My large hands are great for gripping and wielding carpentry tools while my mother's are smaller and adept at braiding. I admire the different ways we've learned to use our hands—especially because we can utilize our distinct qualities to help each other.

Unlike humans, plants do not attach judgment to different appearances. My cactus doesn't mind looking different from my elephant ears; its focus is on its own shape and how it supports the plant's growth. We can heed this ourselves, and let go of the judgment we too often place on our bodies. This is why my experience with my epiphyllum struck me so; its contentious tendrils reminded me of myself. I know what it's like to be the ugly duckling.

MARCUS TALES #9
Losing My Hair

"Give yourself a bald spot" was a game my friends and I played in seventh grade. We wouldn't actually make ourselves bald, but we would part our hair in such a way that we could clearly see our scalps. We found it interesting to compare the color of people's scalps to their faces, as the colors were not always the same. Looking back, this must have been one of those silly things children do when they're exploring who they are and learning about their bodies.

The first time I gave myself a little noogie, my hair parted and revealed my scalp. I ruffled up my hair, the part closed, and it was like nothing had happened. A few days later when I tried again, the "bald spot" I created was harder to close. My hair felt brittle, and my fingers caught something. I pulled my hand away, and in it was a patch of hair . . . with some of my scalp attached.

Over the next few months, more of my hair fell out. None of it grew back. I had perfect attendance at school at the time, and I lost this streak when my school, alarmed at my hair loss, sent me home. They were worried I had the contagious rash ringworm.

Thankfully, I didn't have this rash. It took many trips to the doctor, but my mother and I were able to prove that I was not contagious. Although the shape of the bald patches on my head resembled the symptoms of ringworm, they were the result of something different. In the search for an answer, I had a biopsy that my body did not respond well to. The patches on my head had created soft spots in my skull tissue, similar to those of babies, and the biopsy created fissures between these spots. I literally felt my skull splitting as the fissures connected one soft spot to another. As they did, the tissue of these spots caved in, leading to what looked like craters on my head. I went from having a "normal" smooth head to having a deformed, contorted scalp.

The patches and craters on my head made me stand out among my peers. They teased me by nicknaming me "patch patch" and referred to me as "dalmatian."

The irregularities never went away, so I learned to live with being different. There had been a few times when the teasing bothered me to the point that I was distracted when trying to do my homework, as my energy had been eliminated from trying to keep myself composed. I figured I had to stop it from bothering me so it would not keep me from my responsibilities, and I accepted being the ugly duckling.

Like the curly locks, I was unique to my surroundings, and my appearance was not well liked. I couldn't help this; I didn't have a choice in how my hair fell out and the shapes this created on my head. Deformities and abnormal body shapes are part of the human experience and affect people worldwide.

I went from being treated normally to having people stop making eye contact with me because the abnormality of my head distracted them. As people tried to assess what happened to my head they struggled to look me in the eye. Their assessments frequently turned into judgments without them realizing, as they'd assume I was contagious or gross instead of asking me what had happened. People with even the best of intentions disrespected me with their inability to make and keep eye contact with me. Since going through this trial I've made sure not to do this to others.

To this day, I have to remind myself that it's okay that the shape of my head is unusual. When it comes to the human body, we get used to normalcy and seeing consistent forms around us. When something is abnormal, it's easy to make assumptions and cast judgments instead of considering that there is something we are unaware of. How we make these evaluations is up to us, as we choose how to use our energy. Using a positive mindset, we're more likely to make assessments that help us maintain peace and balance.

Embrace Differences

I have planted caladiums of all colors and varieties in my garden. Some are a translucent white with pale green veins, and others are a deep berry with a lighter pink trim. The caladiums with maroon red leaves and teal green streaks look nothing like the others in terms of color, but they all can be identified by the shape of their leaves.

Every tangible thing has shape and form. Shape, like color, is one physical characteristic we use to tell things apart. Because all forms have a purpose, no shape is better than another. I admire how large my elephant ears grow to be, but I don't expect my caladiums to reach the same height and width. They require different nutrients and amounts of water, thrive in different seasons, and flower in different conditions. They are different plants, and each serves a different purpose in my garden.

Learning to embrace the shape of each plant means appreciating the plant for what it is. If I spent time treating the caladiums as if they were elephant ears, I would waste my energy. The caladiums would probably die, and if they survived, they would still never adopt the form of elephant ears. The same is true for us: by

embracing all parts of our physical selves, we can appreciate and respect our bodies without judgment.

I pined over silver satin pothos for months before
I bought a few cuttings on the internet. Among my
unrooted cuttings was a massive leaf unlike the others. I figured it had been one of the more mature and
healthier cuttings from the mother plant, and with
proper care, the other cuttings would grow to match it.
I later found and bought a silver satin plant in a local
store, and I wondered when its leaves would begin to
grow in size like the large cutting. It turned out that
the unique cutting was not just unique in its size—it
was a different species of plant! It has the same color
pattern and similar texture to my silver satin pothos,
but grows thicker vines and bigger leaves. The leaves
of my silver satin will never become that large, because
the plant simply does not grow in that shape.

Assumptions can be harmful. I assumed my silver satin could and would grow larger with the right
care, and this led me to stunt its growth and weaken
its leaves. It never occurred to me that the two plants
were different. We are prone to making this mistake
with people in several ways. We may look at someone,
evaluate their physical characteristics, and assume we
know their ethnicity, ability, or health, when humans
are far more complex than how we appear.

To me, self-acceptance means freeing myself of assumptions as they relate to my own features. We cannot change some aspects of ourselves, such as height, hair texture, or complexion. Spending my time yearning to change these things about myself is to undermine the parts of myself I should respect and appreciate. Assuming certain features are better or worse than others can cost me time and energy and lead me to stagnate in my own growth.

As much as I've wanted to be six foot six and a couple hundred pounds heavier, that is not the form I have. I may not be able to dunk as easily as some of my taller cousins, but coming to appreciate my form led me to harness my strength, agility, and speed. Where I might struggle to reach for something on a top shelf, my cousin has to duck to walk through doorways. Each of our forms has strengths and weaknesses; learning to maximize our strengths aids us in managing our energy. Instead of spending time on my toes reaching for something high above me, I can accept I'm not tall enough to grab it and should save my energy by getting a stool.

Textures

Nature's Reminder to
Be in the Moment

The fourth core element of physical fitness is understanding the ways we are affected by stimulus. Our bodies have the unique ability to experience sensations around us through touch, sight, sound, taste, and smell. I personally have sensitivity to texture in particular. I didn't realize this until I was well into adulthood, but stimulating one of my senses provokes the stimulation of others and emotional responses. As odd as it sounds, my body responds with emotions to the textures I feel with my fingers, and sometimes tastes and smells. It varies depending on what, where, and when I'm touching something.

Not all of us are as sensitive to texture. Some are more affected by sudden drops in temperature or high-pitched sounds, and others by the air quality. Pay attention to your body and senses: What makes you feel good? What causes you discomfort? These small physical responses to the things around us often have bigger consequences on our overall well-being and state than we realize. For instance, some people are put on edge by windy days. The physical stimulation like the sound of leaves, irregular pattern of pressure on the skin from the wind, and changing images outside the window from trees moving impact their entire mindset throughout the day. I have one friend whose knuckles severely dry out as soon as she is exposed to temperatures below 60 degrees so she must give them extra moisturizer on colder days.

We often overlook these sensations when we think of our well-being, but they can contribute to our health and happiness or disrupt our balance. I see this in my plants all the time. I have a plant hanging in my kitchen window: One side faces the outdoors, and the other my indoors. After a couple months of healthy growth, I noticed the side facing the sunlight had grown considerably more than the other. I turned the plant around and within a couple weeks, the growth evened out.

This is a more obvious example of the ways my plants are affected by stimuli, but something that many amateur indoor plant enthusiasts don't realize is the potent effect of a slight change in temperature. Having around 150 plants inside comes with some labor, and paying attention to the weather changes is part of the job. The temperature dips enough for me to turn my heat on at the end of November, and some of my plants will shrivel to conserve energy until I change the temperature of my house to match their ideal conditions. Failing to realize the subtle ways my plants respond to stimuli could limit their potential or even threaten their health.

Like plants, our bodies have varying textures just as they do colors and shapes, but let's focus on how our bodies *respond* to texture, and stimuli in general. We often overlook these sensations when we think of our well-being, but they can contribute to our health and happiness or disrupt our balance.

Our bodies experience sensation through textures, temperature changes, light fluctuations, and other stimuli. Let's listen to our bodies, and learn what promotes wellness in our bodies and what compromises it. These same stimuli also serve as reminders for us to stay present if we're distracted so we can keep ourselves focused on growth and well-being. Let's use stimulus to strengthen the connection between our mind and body, and let our peace support our balance.

Listen to Your Body

What would happen if a plant's roots and leaves didn't listen to each other and work together? The leaves might try to grow without the support of the roots, and the plant would perish from exhaustion. If we don't listen to our bodies, we put ourselves at risk for harm and uneven growth.

For most of my life, I wasn't aware of my texture sensitivity. I'd experience strange reactions to fabric and paper, and try my best to feel comfortable again. I struggled as a child to ignore the pain and discomfort I felt regularly, but I had no idea what caused this response. This meant I couldn't articulate it to other people, so I thought I was abnormal and weird and kept it to myself. I did my best to handle it myself, and years later I now understand that I have some sensitivity to dryness, paper, and fabrics.

I learned something from my texture sensitivity: only we can listen to our bodies, as only our minds are connected to them. If the body is signaling something to the mind, we should listen. I didn't want to look odd in front of my childhood peers so I'd try to ignore my body's signals, but I'd often wind up harming myself. A pair of pants gave me such an itch that I drew blood scratching myself as I tried to cope with the sensation.

Don't let the judgments of others skew your ability to listen to your body. If you hear a bothersome high-pitched ringing that nobody else can, don't ignore it because others are unaffected. You might be able to hear a wider range of frequency and need to learn to work with this heightened sense. There are infinite different stimuli that affect all of us differently—nobody responds to the same stimuli the same way.

Our balance depends on our ability to listen to our bodies and know when something is off, what part of us needs tending, and how we can resolve any issues. Practice listening to your body by taking time to focus your mind on different parts of your body: your hands, elbows, shoulders, knees, head. Learn each part and strengthen your mind's connection to them so you can easily understand their responses to stimuli.

If you feel your leaves curl and burn at the ends, you might need some shade—even if the plant next to you doesn't have even a spot of sun damage. If your roots can't grow through the rocky soil in your pot, you may need replanting, regardless if the other plants in the pot are starting to flower. Your body is your vessel for experiencing the world. Trust, respect, and listen to it.

I tested the connection between my mind and body in a youth group activity when I was fourteen. Given my relationship to texture, I wasn't excited about my participation at first but came to appreciate the experience and what it taught me.

MARCUS TALES #10
Feeling in the Dark

We were to put on blindfolds, feel miscellaneous objects or substances, and try to guess what we were touching.

The supervisors made sure our eyes were covered and led us to a table where five unknown materials waited for our identification. My peers felt the mysterious substances before me so I could hear their responses to the unknown entities they touched with their hands. I heard a few screams, and a couple shouts of, "Gross!"

My unease subsided, and intrigue took its place. The responses of my friends and their guesses piqued my interest and I wondered if I'd be able to successfully identify any of the enigmas waiting for me.

We could only use one hand in one container at a time. Some people alternated the hands they used throughout the activity, but I chose to stick with my left so I could be consistent.

I felt my heart beat as I stepped up to the table and plunged my hand into the first container. I felt around, letting my fingers explore what filled the bowl. My mind tried to put together the mystery that my hands investigated, but I couldn't think of anything.

The supervisors cleaned my hand for me and I tried the next one. Another loss. Out of all five, I guessed two correctly: Milk, and spaghetti and meatballs. I failed to identify yogurt and gummy bears, wet dog food and potatoes, and a mix of dry cereal. Thankfully, none of the textures of the foodstuff sparked a strange response from my body and I could enjoy focusing on the task at hand.

Since the youth group meetings I've thought about the connection between the mind and body, and how they work together to navigate through the complexities of the world and of its stimuli. Although I didn't correctly guess every container of matter, I could discern the general textures of what I felt. My body responded differently to each container of matter, and my mind sought understanding. I needed to let my body speak to my mind, and listen.

Do I know what I am interacting with? What is my body telling me about this interaction? I asked myself these questions during this activity and they've stayed with me since this day of youth group. I think we can all stand to ask them of ourselves as we check in with ourselves and practice listening to our bodies.

Stay Present to Keep Your Balance

I consider myself blessed to have grown up outdoors and spent hours upon hours in nature exposed to numerous textures. Lounging in bushy fruit trees, smelling roses and hibiscus, and adventuring through the woods are some of my fondest memories.

Nature isn't always smooth kumquats and scaly gator sightings, though. Sometimes I'd cut my knee tripping over a sharp rock or get a nasty scratch from a fallen branch. If I was particularly unfortunate, I'd encounter what we called "fireweed," commonly known as "stinging nettle," a plant that grows all over north and central Florida. Its looks are deceiving; although it resembles your everyday weed, this one's leaves are covered in venomous tiny hairs that can be lethal to touch.

Well, it's not actually lethal, but the sting it leaves on your skin is brutal. My worst experience with fireweed occurred when I unknowingly fell into a patch of it while playing football. To think, a few touches of this plant and my entire day changed. For the rest of the day, I was consumed with agonizing itching and stinging to the point that I could not think straight. I hope not to relive this pain, but the experience blessed me with a lesson: being present.

Being present, or "in the moment," means we are focused on what we're doing and how we are using our body. We want to be present so we can see problems before they happen, address them as they develop, and make choices to preserve our well-being. I was preoccupied before I played football with my cousins and didn't notice the weed I would soon fall into. I never made that mistake again, and I made a point to stay present in future outdoor activities so I would look for fireweed and other dangers.

We need to be in the moment to truly listen to our bodies; it's essential to improving and using the connection between the mind and body. If we feel our peace slipping or our balance threatened, there's a chance we've let our mind wander too far from our well-being.

It can be easy to get caught up in thoughts or experiences of the past or worries for the future, but our best bet at keeping our balance is listening to our bodies *now* and making choices that take into account what we are experiencing.

A physical stimulus doesn't need to incite pain and discomfort to engage our focus and keep us present. Something pleasant is equally as effective. We need to listen to our bodies to make positive choices for our well-being, but it's easy to forget this when our minds are busy or distracted. We're exposed to more stimuli than ever before between the music we hear every time we visit a shop and the ever increasing prevalence of screens, and we need to be mindful of how we engage with the external forces that stimulate us.

Sometimes we need to tune out these extraneous sounds and lit up screens, but an unfortunate consequence of this mental blockading is a growing numbness, a distracted state of being. Be in the moment even when you are intentionally tuning out a stimulus so you don't miss essential information and compromise your body.

Being present helps us maintain our physical well-being in other ways, too, such as when we need to evaluate our colors or assess the different layers of our bodies.

Layers

A Comprehensive View of Physical Well-Being

The fifth core component of our physical fitness is knowing that the different parts of ourselves come together as one, and we best care for ourselves when we pay attention to each part. I do this by thinking of my body and experience in layers. When a problem develops in my body, I need to determine where it began: Is it in my bones, muscles, organs, or veins? Then I need to consider when it began and what I can do to stop it from growing into a greater issue.

Aloe vera is a succulent that is known widely for its

medicinal benefits. I love the look and versatility of this plant. I'd nursed an aloe plant from three-inch pups to two-and-a-half-foot leaves that were wide and thick with gel. Over the course of its growth, I observed the relationship between the layers of the plant. Aloe has three major layers: the inside gel, a protective skin encasing the gel, and an outer rind. I used this plant for my skin throughout its growth, and I noticed a consistency every time I broke off a piece. The layers were always proportional to one another and the size of the plant. This struck me because it reminded me that all the layers within all things must work together to sustain growth.

I've observed a fascinating change in one of the aloe vera plants my mother sent me from Florida. In its life, it's gone from being one of several pups to becoming a mother and yielding twelve new plants. The aloe has survived torrential rainstorms, unprecedentedly cold temperatures, and blazing heat—and it appears to have grown stronger. While dozens of my other aloe plants died over the past year, this is one of four to remain alive and growing in my garden. I've come to change how I care for it: it needs less maintenance, fewer soil changes, and it doesn't need to be moved around the yard as much. It seems to me that the aloe became hardier as a result of its experiences.

Like the aloe, our bodies are layered, too, with literal layers to our physical form that give us distinction and character. We cannot maintain balance without maintaining every layer of ourselves. The physical layers of our bodies, our muscles, veins, organs, and bones, are equally important to our physical fitness, and the different parts of bodies work as one: to ignore any part of ourselves is to neglect the entirety of our body and compromise its ability to function. If we develop a pain in our leg after a workout, how do we know if we're dealing with inflamed bone tissue or a strained muscle? Conceptualizing our body in layers helps us consider the various parts of ourselves so we can better address problems and maximize our potential.

Our experiences are also layered; they build on each other to create the story of our life. What I do today shapes my tomorrow, and my tomorrow could affect my next week, and my next week the next year. This is why I advocate we practice hobbies, habits, and routines to nurture our bodies. The better I care for myself today, the better condition I'll be in tomorrow. Take time every day to listen to your body: Are you satisfying its needs? Is it unwell and requires extra attention? The sooner we can answer such questions, the better we can prepare ourselves for long-term growth.

Learn the Layers of our Bodies

Our bodies consist of several layers, including skin, muscles, bones. Like those in the aloe plant, each layer serves a unique purpose but works closely with the others. Recognizing I have to care for each layer was another stage in my understanding of how to manage my energy. Neglecting to nurture each layer creates an imbalance in our bodies that can manifest in illness, fatigue, or injury. If I don't consume sufficient nutrients, my skin will become inconsistent in its color, shape, and texture.

Developing hobbies, habits, and routines to tend to each layer of our body helps us keep our balance and work efficiently as one. I care for the layers of myself in a variety of ways, including eating well for bone health, stretching for my muscles, and using moisturizer for my skin. This might sound simple, but taking care of each individual level of my body makes a difference. I notice that when I don't stretch regularly, I develop muscle cramps. These siphon my energy and make it harder for me to care for the other parts of myself.

A common problem we face when caring for our plants is figuring which part of a plant is affected when problems arise. Discoloration on the leaves of a "Florida Beauty" could be the result of a complication with its roots or an infection on its stem—not the leaves alone. Thinking of the plant in layers helps us isolate the issue. In gardening, the most basic question we ask ourselves when looking at an ailing plant is: What does it need? Water, light, new soil? Now let's consider ourselves: What are our roots, bark, leaves, flowers? When we feel fatigued or unwell, what layer needs attention? What will it need to feel better—a glass of water, a snack, a nap, a walk? Separate the layers of yourself to target a problem and find a solution.

MARCUS TALES #11
Cost of Fashion

During my high school years, I started taking my style seriously and started matching my outfits by color. I needed shoes to complete my outfits so I saved up some money and bought four different-colored pairs of shoes that I could rotate between my outfits. They weren't great quality, but I didn't know this at the time as I'd never had access to anything better.

My days in high school were long; between the

commute to school, classes, and theater, I was in my shoes all day. It didn't matter if I was exercising, set building, or studying—I was going to look and feel great. Thinking back to those years, I was definitely more concerned with style than functionality of the shoes. *They don't feel too good*, I thought to myself a few times, *but they look amazing.* By the time I was a senior, I'd worn down the soles of all four pairs to the point of nonexistence.

I didn't realize the impact this would have on my body until I developed unbearable shin splints. I sat down in the scene shop of my high school to rub my shins when someone approached me, noticing my pain, and asked a question that would change my life: "When was the last time you changed your shoes?"

Shin splints weren't the only problem I experienced. Callouses developed on my feet from the lack of support in the shoes. My feet and ankles hurt all the time when I wore these shoes. Focusing on fashion and neglecting to replace my shoes sooner compromised the integrity of my well-being.

The callouses did not just *appear*, and neither did the shin splints. They developed over time. The skin of my outer layer formed callouses to protect my feet in response to the constant friction of ruined material. The internal layers of my muscles, tendons, and bones were stressed from the lack of support. Every day that

I cycled between those four pairs of shoes contributed to the problems my body experienced. I would have saved myself a good deal of agony and frustration had I listened to the small discomforts that built up to major pain.

I had to take time tending to the different layers to heal completely, and acknowledge that I would have had less work and recovery if I'd stopped to assess my body before the problem took me off my feet.

Learn the Layers of Experience

In addition to using this layer mindset to address different parts of our physical selves and their needs, we can think about the layers of our life that impact our physical well-being.

On the journey of life, we meet with situations and experiences that layer one upon the other. I think of these as snapshots, one for every day. Each day, our layers thicken and build up, adding to the depth of our experience. As we reflect on our lives and our choices, we need to be attentive to our layers—the snapshot of what's happening in that moment, and how the experiences stack up to create a story.

In this way, every day is significant because of how each adds to our depth. How we use our time matters, and this is why we should focus on hobbies, habits, and routines that encourage peace and balance. What we do today affects our tomorrow, so implement hobbies, habits, and routines that encourage peace and balance if you want to see it in your future. If a problem develops in your physical fitness, don't wait to investigate. Every day you wait to evaluate your colors, look for changes in your shape, and consider that how stimuli affects you increases the depth of the problem. The issue will continue growing over time and could be harder to resolve than when it began.

I had a grapevine growing in the back corner of my garden for a few years, and every day I watched it grow and fill more space in my garden. As time passed, the plants in other layers of the same area grew and expanded until they shaded the grapevine from the light.

One of the things I appreciate most about plants is how they will grow however they can to find sunlight or water, and that's what my grapevine did. Covered by the other plants and pushed against my fence, it grew upward until it connected with my oleander tree and climbed its way to a free spot in the sun. One day, I noticed it had yellowed from its top to its bottom.

I hadn't been able to spend time in my garden to check the plants every day, so I didn't see the yellowing until enough time had passed for it to consume the plant.

To address the issue that was causing the discoloration, I had to cut back the leaves of several plants in the lower layers in front of the grapevine. These plants had thrived, and I was surprised by the depth I had to cut through to reach the vine. Finally, I reached the source of a problem: a weed suffocating the roots and the stem of the plant. With every day that I failed to address the issue, the depth of the problem grew. Had I found the weed before it grew large enough to affect my grapevine, I could have saved this plant as well as the plants I had to cut back from stifled growth.

This can happen to us, too. A weed can show up in our life as a problem we don't notice or we choose to ignore. After a week of pain in my shoulder, I took time to stretch and work out what I thought was a kink. It occurred to me that I'd had some lower back pain a couple weeks earlier and I realized the injuries might have a connection, especially because my back pain grew out of a chest injury that I'd incurred a couple months prior. Busy with work, I admit that I did not properly attend to the chest problem and instead let my body compensate for my weakened chest by compromising other parts of myself. Every day that I did not address the problem at the root, it affected more of my body.

It only takes a moment out of one day for a problem to develop into something that could extend into weeks, months, and years. Failing to address a problem in a part of ourselves today, be it in a layer of our body or a layer of our being, could create problems in other parts of ourselves tomorrow. To keep this from happening, I encourage creating routines to promote wellness in every layer of ourselves regularly.

12

Design

Bring Colors, Shapes, Textures, and Layers Together

Preserving our physical well-being requires attention to our entire body. This is especially important when we're healing, the process of recovering from an ailment. We'll experience troubles in life that tax our minds and bodies, and we need to use our new skills to evaluate and address physical well-being. Additionally, I think we can all stand to heal from the negative and often harmful ideals of health we've been presented. Now that we have a comprehensive understanding of ourselves—our colors, shapes, textures, and layers—we can apply our knowledge to our gardens, hobbies, habits, and routines.

We should aim to grow from hardship like the aloe I mentioned in Chapter 11. To heal in both our bodies and our mindsets, we need to let go of negativity. Grounded in positivity, we can focus on healing toward growth.

The garden teaches us the importance of rethinking our ideas of physical health: we bloom and flourish when we focus more on what contributes to our growth and balance, and pay less attention to appearance or how much weight we can lift. Tune out harmful and damaging ideas of physical well-being, and listen to your body. We are all different, and our bodies reflect this. Familiarize yourself with your particular colors, shapes, textures, and layers. Then, focus on appreciating them.

Design with Intention: Let Go of Negativity

I have a six-by-eight-foot porch leading into my home. When I was designing it, I kept colors, shapes, textures, and layers of my plants in mind. My goal was to create a calm, healing space that left all who passed through it with a sense of tranquility. When I modeled it, I had decontamination zones in mind; the colors, shapes, textures, and layers would wash over people who walked through, cleansing them of their day-to-day stresses.

Placing my plants in layers from the ground to the ceiling ensured there was luscious greenery everywhere the eye looked. I used pothos vines to drape down the brick walls, contrasting their bright green, smooth, oval leaves with the rustic red, rough rectangles of the bricks. I then filled the top layer of the porch with only a few hanging plants. I used plant stands of various shapes and heights, topped with bromeliads and begonias, to fill the middle and lower layers of my porch.

Using colors, shapes, textures, and layers led me to design a beautiful space and eventually caused me to reflect on the parts of my body and how they come together. My porch is a unique and vibrant collection of various parts and pieces, similar to myself. I also care for every plant in my porch individually just as I do the different parts of myself; I don't wash my hair the same way I wash my feet. I placed each plant according to how much sunlight it needs and water them accordingly. Every plant has specific needs, and treating them as if they were the same would leave with me a porch of lost plants and a broken heart.

It's much easier to focus on our personal fitness after freeing ourselves of unnecessary pressure, urges to compare ourselves to others, and trying to fit a mold that doesn't work for us. Healing and growth are different for everyone. Fitness doesn't need to be stressful or something we dread. Have fun! Experiment with your activities and fitness routines, listen to your body, and take notes. What makes you feel strong? Do you feel refreshed after going for a walk or a run? Is that body ache you often feel the result of positive hard work, or from overexertion in a workout you don't enjoy?

Use this information to work with intention so each lesson is able to support the next. Consider the benefits of thinking of the body as a plant—as something made of colors, shapes, textures, and layers. This helps us create hobbies, habits, and routines that sustain our growth, keep our balance, and heal. Through this technique, we deepen our understanding of our physical fitness, strengthen the connection between the mind and body, increasing peace in our mind and balance in the body, thereby improving our well-being.

I designed my porch to heal people before they entered my house because I wanted people to leave their negativity on the other side of my door. Guests always comment on its effect, and I am proud of my work. Tending to my multidimensional porch reminds me of how important it is to let go of negativity and care for the entirety of my being while healing, which was something I was forced to confront after I broke my arm at seventeen years old.

MARCUS TALES #12
Set Building

The fall musical of my senior year of high school was *The Wiz*, and I was the technical director for the production as well as a main role. We started set building in the summer before the school year started to ensure everything would be finished on schedule. I was part of an exclusive theater program at a magnet high school, and there was an expectation of quality. People came from all over Orlando to watch our productions.

My friend and I were working late one night to finish the larger and more complicated set pieces as the show approached. Only a few weeks away from the show, I was waking up early and going to sleep late on top of a full day of summer classes, camps, and rehearsal, and living over an hour away from school. Needless to say, this expenditure of energy took a toll on me as I was not doing enough to replenish myself.

The lack of energy led me to make a thoughtless mistake in the process of construction; the mistake occurred when I was working on a unit while suspended sixteen feet in the air. I fell to the ground, landed on my left arm, and wound up with a compound fracture. I'll spare you the gory details, but my forearm bone was visibly broken.

Because of how I broke it, the bone split through other layers of my arm: muscle, nerves, and skin. Rods were implanted to stabilize the shape of the healing bone in surgery, and my skin was stapled shut to seal the wound. This happened in 2004; nearly two decades later, signs of the injury linger.

After the surgery left discolored scarring on both sides of my arm, I found myself with some negative thoughts about self-worth. A bumpy texture remains where the staples once held my skin together, and the shape of my forearm is uneven because of how the bone fused back together and how my muscles were displaced. Having torn through and damaged multiple layers of my arm, it's taken constant effort to keep it strong enough to use. For years, I couldn't lift more than ten or fifteen pounds with it. With practice, I've gotten some of my strength back.

Every stage of recovery requires patience and nurturance. I was determined to heal my arm to the best possible condition, and this required letting go of negativity and caring for every layer of it. Years of ointments and topical treatments eased the pain, softened the texture, and lightened the dark color of the scar. Constant stretching has realigned my muscles and helped my arm not only feel better, but look less misshapen. The experience showed me the benefits of solution-focused positive thinking, stretching, strengthening, and moisturizing all my body, and I am now far more physically balanced than I was before the injury.

I was able to recover from my injury by implementing conscious and deliberate routines. Finding a new balance after a terribly disruptive accident or injury takes time and effort, but it's possible when we're willing to search for solutions, adapt, and experiment. Thinking of my body holistically and considering the shapes, colors, textures, and layers of myself has continued to help me recover from other injuries and stay balanced.

Healing Through a Growth Mindset

As long as there is life in a plant, it will do everything it can to grow. It may be no more than an inch-long stalk or a leaf broken from a vine, but if presented with the right conditions, it will grow. I've nursed countless of dying plants back to health and seen this to be true. I attribute this to plants not getting in the way of their own growth, which is a problem I commonly see with people.

Our growth can feel most vulnerable when we're healing, not only from injury or illness but also from harmful mindsets or bad experiences. We are constantly presented with ideals: the best physique, the perfect diet for rapid results, the only way to embody the epitome of fitness. Let's look to our plants for guidance and remember that every one of us is unique. The lauded ideals may not work for us, and they don't need to. A quality physical fitness will look different for all of us. By using our skills of observation and awareness, listening to our body, and paying attention to our needs, we can determine the best way to care for ourselves.

Healing our mentality supports us so we can heal our bodies. Throughout our lifetimes, we will experience illness and injury to varying degrees. Healing is a process and, depending on our experiences, is different for everyone. Some of us are born with injury and illness that will never go away, and others may only break a bone or stub a toe. The act of maintaining our physical well-being is a form of healing. Regardless of what state we are in or what is ailing us, we can create hobbies, habits, and routines to manage our physical fitness and support our well-being.

It's important to note that healing takes time, and we shouldn't rush the process. Design hobbies, habits, and routines that will allow you to accomplish realistic goals as you work toward something larger. When we don't see the progress we want when we want it, it's easy to give up—and get in the way of our own growth. The dying plants I rescued didn't fill their pots with new life in a day; it typically took the better part of a year for the signs of decline to disappear. Rushing to heal can actually set us back as we may open ourselves to infection or additional harm. Life is a process with many layers and stages, and we must respect them all. Be patient and thorough, and address each layer of yourself.

Last, design hobbies, habits, and routines that remove judgment from your process. Comparing yourself to others or trying to emulate an ideal that won't work for you is a waste of your energy. With peace and balance, you can free yourself of unnecessary pressure, find clarity, and determine the best way for you to heal.

As you go through this process of restoration, remember to treat yourself with kindness, patience, and positivity. Be kind to yourself so you can be forgiving, and use mistakes as opportunities to learn. Be patient as you experience changes and attempt to heal; you must go through every stage to mend every layer of yourself fully. Last, but not least, be positive so you can face any challenges or adversity with your best self.

In Sum

The more I practiced positivity and peace in my thinking, the easier it became to connect with my physical fitness. I began seeing my body through a new lens, one that focused on my energy, and thus my well-being, removing judgment, my body's responses, and healing. I learned my body is a collection of parts that come together and work as one. These concepts moved me away from shame and frustration and closer to acceptance and growth, and healthier well-being.

We can't do anything to improve our physical fitness without first devoting effort to our energy. How are we using our energy? How are we wasting it? Learning to manage our energy helps us keep pace through the day and prevent exhaustion. When I find myself losing rhythm, I return to my breath and center myself.

Plants teach us that all our colors, shapes, textures, and layers are what make us unique. Use color as a tool to evaluate the state of your well-being. Let your shape remind you that there's no place for judgment in practicing physical fitness. Regardless of our form, we all have skills we can use to contribute to our community and environment. Listen, because nobody can hear your body better than you. Use your body's responses to stimuli, like texture, to stay engaged and in the moment. This will make it easier to distinguish between your mental and physical feelings as you go through your days. Think of yourself in layers so you can identify the source of an ailment and figure out how to care for yourself.

With a comprehensive understanding of who and what we are, we can design hobbies, habits, and routines for our well-being. We can heal and continue moving forward in a direction of growth.

Be Diligent in Your Care,
and Grow with a Plant

In this activity, we'll keep ourselves accountable for our care of our physical fitness by caring for a plant.

1. Head to your local plant store or nursery. Let yourself wander, observing all the beautiful greenery the center has to offer. There's no need to rush the process. Your goal is to find a plant that calls to you—maybe you admire its colors or its shape, or perhaps you're drawn to its scent. Whatever the magic quality is, you'll know when you've found your new companion.

2. When you've found your plant, think of what you'll need to do to help it flourish. Do you have to clear off a windowsill for it, or remove some weeds from a plot of land? What tools will you need to accomplish this task? If you're unsure of what conditions it needs, ask an expert from the facility or do some research.

3. Once you've brought the plant home, it's time to start experimenting. If it's a houseplant, you may need to (gently) move it around your space before you find its ideal spot. Pay attention to how it responds to light and water, and your routine of care. Learn what your plant needs.

4. Every time you check on your plant, water it, move it, and so on, use the opportunity as a reminder to check in with yourself. How is your energy? Have you been consistent with your growth-focused hobbies, habits, and routines? Let caring for your plant keep you accountable for your care of yourself.

Note: Even I find myself so consumed by work and projects that I forget to stretch, eat certain nutrients, and get sufficient rest. I've noticed that when I neglect myself, I generally fail my plants. If more than one of my plants declines, it's typically a sign that I've lost rhythm with my routines, and I take the reminder to get back on track.

PART THREE

Spiritual Awareness

Find Harmony by Nurturing Connection

What is the secret to a healthy garden?

As more people visit my garden and see pictures of it online, I'm met with inquiries about how I've created such a space. If there is any secret, it's that my garden and I grow alongside each other. Nurturing myself allows me to nourish my land and all the plants and creatures that share it with me. My garden energizes and calms me in turn, and I cherish our relationship. It helps me maintain peace in my mind, balance in my body, and harmony in my spirit.

In Part I, we set up a garden in our minds to grow a positive mindset and find peace. In Part II, we thought about how we can improve our physical fitness and balance by learning from the physical characteristics and experiences of plants. Now, we need to think of how individual plants come together to create a garden.

Nobody who visits my garden today would recognize it had they seen it when I first moved into my house. It was barren, a giant patch of dirt with a couple trees and some persistent weeds. Over the course of a few years, I prepared my space, planted seeds, learned to compost, and watched the yard transform. The garden began to take on a life of its own.

Many of my initial experiments and gardening happened in the circular bed surrounding my Arizona ash tree. Purple queen, elephant ears, caladiums of all colors, sword grass, and canna bulbs grew and made their presence known, presenting me with the opportunity to learn about each of them, with all their nuances and needs. I looked at their colors and shapes, observed their responses to the climate, and admired the visual layers they created together.

Then, a thought struck me: the individual plants shared the same soil, coming together to form a community. I saw how the plants interacted with one another and how they affected the growing community around my ash tree. I saw how they worked together and developed a balance that I could easily disrupt with thoughtless decisions like using poor topsoil. If one plant declined, the others were liable to follow suit. They were intricately connected, and part of something greater than each plant alone.

Little did I know, my process of caring and learning in the garden turned into a spiritual practice that gave my life a newfound meaning, providing me a sense of fulfillment and a connection to something greater than myself.

Gardening became my favorite practice to nourish my spirit, one I welcomed into my routine with open arms. The spirit needs just as much attention as the mind and body, though it's easy to forget this in our fast-paced modern age.

Our spirit is the charge inside us that we refer to as *Life*. It's our small portion of the greater force that is Life in all living things, the power source that fuels us until we transition to death. I believe the spirit is neither inherently good nor evil, it simply *is*. As we aim for peace in our mind and balance in our body, we seek harmony in our spirit, the state of being composed, alert, and engaged. We need harmony to maximize our potential, and we can incorporate spiritual practices into our hobbies, habits, and routines to accomplish this.

We all have a spirit, but we must choose to develop the tool of spiritual awareness, consciousness of the Life inside us, who we share it with and how we are affected by our community and environment. Like the plants growing around my Arizona ash tree, we are not alone and are affected by those around us.

I believe we should develop our spiritual awareness for two key reasons. First, awareness of the spirit is essential to the foundation of our well-being because it ties our mind and body together. Second, it determines how we share our spirit with the life around us—how we build strong communities and foster healthy environments. We see this in our garden every day: there is a shared greater force with all plants, insects, worms, birds, and other creatures. The way pollinators and flowers depend on each other for growth shows us that nothing lives alone in the garden.

Where we grow and who we grow with are the major external factors in our growth. Our spiritual awareness is essential to evaluating our communities and environments, understanding how they affect us, and learning how we can support them. Peace, balance, and harmony enable us to nurture our communities and environments to help other beings grow as well, yielding a collective balance we can all enjoy.

SPIRITUAL METAPHOR

Sharing the Garden

For the first time in years, you decide to revisit the village you entered when you made it through the brush. The pressure to meet your quota kept you confined to your garden. Now that every plant has declined, you accept you cannot produce enough and you might as well go for a walk. There is nothing more for you to lose.

As you walk through the village, you are shocked to see how much has changed. More people must have carved their way to the community, because huts, houses, and gardens fill the space where trees and foliage once grew. The environment you originally moved to no longer exists. Looking around the transformed settlement, you wonder: *Where are the people?*

You stop at the nearest house and knock on the door. Nobody answers. You move on.

Several houses later, someone finally answers the door.

"I can't talk right now, I'm working in my garden." The person says this bluntly before closing the door on you. The intensity in their eyes strikes you because it reminds you of yourself and your dedication to your garden. The door shuts, and you remember being so concerned with your own garden that when someone knocked on your door, you sent them away so you could keep working.

Did I sound and look like this person? What if I'd stopped when someone came to see me? you ask yourself. Maybe you would have seen the decline of the garden before it took over and destroyed everything.

You knock on the door again. The same person answers and looks angry to be disturbed a second time.

"I told you I'm busy. I need to get back to work in my garden. I need to meet my quota." As they say "quota," you hear both the pressure and defeat you felt day in and day out working with your plants.

Seeing an opportunity to share information you know with someone who could benefit from it, you say, "I know—I'm a gardener, too. I think I can help you." Before they can shut the door on you again, you hastily add, "I won't get in the way of your production."

They say nothing and beckon for you to follow them inside. When you enter the garden, you see the leaves on the trellised vines are beginning to yellow. Mites are eating at caladiums, and debris has started to accumulate on the ground.

In the middle of the garden is a thriving vibrant rosebush, as beautiful as yours had been before its decline.

This is what your garden must have looked like in its

early stages of neglect. You never stopped to get rid of the mites or tend to the vines. In the interest of time, you sent away everyone who came to your door.

"While you work on the rosebush, I'm going to wash these caladiums free of the mites. I'll have to cut some leaves away, but the plant should grow back healthier."

The other gardener grunts, barely looking at you, and bends over the rosebush with a hand on their lower back. You touch yours, remembering how much it hurt to stand up straight for the first time in as long as you could remember.

You both work in silence for an hour.

"When was the last time you watered the vines on your trellis?" you ask.

The other gardener jumps back and looks at you wildly, as if they forgot you were there.

"I don't have time for that plant anymore. It stopped growing and I could no longer include it in my quota. I have to focus on the rosebush."

"I thought the same thing when I was tending to my garden. Now, I have nothing else left, and my rosebush is dying. The plant stopped growing because I stopped caring for it." You guide the other gardener around the garden and show them what you did to the caladiums and where you cleaned up debris.

"I didn't realize at the time, but every plant in the

garden is connected. They are a community. If I had cleaned the beds regularly, I could have both stretched my back and kept the plants alive. Instead, the infestation in one of my beds expanded to the others. The debris piled up and stifled everything else. I ignored them until they died, all while straining my body on the rosebush. This environment is leading you to hurt yourself. Don't you feel that pain in your back?"

The other gardener is speechless for a moment, touching their back and becoming aware of the soreness.

"If you hadn't insisted on helping me, I would never have known. Others have come to my door and I closed it on all of them. I've been trying every day to meet my quota, and I started focusing entirely on my rosebush. I thought it was the easiest way to complete my work, but I now see that I've neglected every other plant, and myself."

"I never let anybody in either, and now all my plants are gone. I have nothing for the collectors. If we fix up this garden, you'll have more than enough for your quota. Let me help you so you can avoid losing your garden, too."

You stay with the gardener until everything has been cleaned up. When you are finished, they give you enough cuttings and seeds to give to the collectors and to rebuild your own garden.

We all have the potential to become these gardeners—so focused on our priorities that we isolate ourselves. We need each other, but it can be hard to hear someone who is offering their help when we're distracted. Community and environment are great resources—we have to respect those tools and benefit from the support they provide or we are likely to repeat the mistakes of our forefathers. Spiritual awareness helps us to avoid repeating those mistakes by keeping us focused on maximizing our potential and seizing the opportunities around us.

The Self

Tend to Each Plant Individually

think of tending to my spirit as caring for a single plant because I am an individual with potential to grow and, given the right care, endless opportunities to flower. I need harmony within myself before I can fully bloom, and once my petals open, I can share my harmony with the other plants and creatures that share my soil.

We can use spiritual practices to increase our harmony and to support our peace and balance, as well as connect with the greater force of Life. I don't think there are strict parameters to what defines a spiritual practice; in essence, it's anything we do to nurture our spirit, improve our spiritual awareness, and focus on our harmony—keeping us composed, alert, and engaged. I've tried a variety of techniques and found my favorite practices are gardening, exercising my inspiration, harnessing my vibration, practicing stillness, meditating, and praying.

Spiritual harmony means we are composed, alert, and engaged. Being composed means we are in control of our mind and body and able to address any issues that arise between them. We aim to be alert so we can stay in the moment and maintain our composure. To be engaged is to be disciplined, motivated, and assertive in interactions with others.

How do we become composed, alert, and engaged? We develop our composure by working on our mental health and physical fitness; I've found great success by following the information I shared in Parts I and II. Alertness comes from taking time to observe cause and effect, and seeing the relationships that connect everything to everything else. What are the consequences of our choices and actions? How are we impacted by the actions of others and the movement of the world around us? Finally, we become engaged by practicing discipline in our minds and bodies, courage when facing adversity, and self-motivation when interacting with others.

I felt a change in my spirit after expanding my plant collection from the indoors to my backyard. The process of transition gave me new responsibilities and routines to develop. My work limited my time at home, and I needed practices for stress reduction and grounding. Thankfully, I could accomplish my gardening responsibilities and exercise my mind, body, and spirit at the same time. Working in the garden grounded me. The days I woke up before work to water my plants gave me calming energy and a sense of composure I could carry with me throughout my day. I was less annoyed and enjoyed myself more.

As the year continued, my schedule grew increasingly hectic. Waking up early in the morning before work became a struggle as my discipline waned, and the middle of the night was the only time I found to work in my garden and renew my composure. This routine prompted a decline in my energy and ability to maintain my composure. Unsurprisingly, my plants suffered as a result. The days were too hot for them without a morning sprinkle; watering them at night proved insufficient, and much of the water evaporated before the sun hit its peak in the sky.

Seeking more harmony in my life, I decided to adjust my routines and wake up early so I could better manage my well-being and the health of my garden. I had a problem to solve, so I used my alertness to note the cause and effect of my choices, and to inform my future choices. I focused on discipline and self-motivation so I could better engage with myself and my plants until we all began to grow once more. This is the importance of spiritual awareness: knowing the impact of our choices on ourselves and on the communities and environments around us, and how to make choices that benefit us all.

Let's care for our spirit and enhance our spiritual awareness with spiritual practices. I don't use every technique in this chapter every day—I check in with myself and determine what I need to do to keep my harmony. If you're new to incorporating such activities into your routine, I recommend starting small and giving yourself room to explore. Don't worry if your approach or experience in meditation or prayer is different from mine; we're different people with different needs and experiences. Enjoy the time you set aside for your wellness, and use the opportunity to grow.

Inspire Your Spirit

Every plant is brimming with inspiration, and I see this in the varying ways they grow. Vines are inspired to climb, shrubs to bush, and grass to spread across the land. We can point to a multitude of reasons why plants grow differently, and I believe their innate inspiration is one of them.

As we discussed in Part I, our *inspirations* are urges of the spirit, often referred to as our passions. They compel us in powerful ways. Inspiration is not necessarily beneficial or harmful—it's simply a compulsion of our spirit we feel drawn to pursue. Why am I inspired to garden? Why is my mother drawn to caring for the unwell? I cannot explain why we have the inspirations we do, but I've learned we need to be conscious of them all the same. This can be challenging, as we often feel a sense of vigor and enthusiasm when we are engaged in our passions or inspirations. They tend to give us our most rewarding experiences. Inspiration is a powerful tool, providing motivation even in depressing times.

Connecting with inspiration becomes a spiritual practice when it helps us improve and maintain a composed, alert, and engaged state of being. This means our inspiration helps us control our mind, see patterns in our experiences and the world around us, and find fulfillment. One should finish a spiritual practice refreshed and rejuvenated. All of us have inspiration inside us at all times. If you feel like you have no inspiration, you may be unaware of it or too distracted to know of it. The other practices I discuss in this chapter are great ways to overcome distraction and reconnect with your inspiration.

As we experience inspiration, and pursue it as a spiritual practice, we must discern if the pursuit of our inspiration comes at the cost of our well-being, community, and environment. Feeling inspired to act in ways that disturb or harm the well-being of ourselves or others is not a reason to follow the urge or act on it. You may feel inspired to grow a canopy of leaves that shade the sun-thirsty plants beneath you even though it would cut them off from their life source. If this happens, focus on hobbies, habits, and routines that feed your spirit without creating unnecessary problems.

Furthermore, we cannot let practicing our inspiration come at the cost of our own well-being and must balance our passions with our mind and body. Are your vines growing out of your planter, and if so, where are they going? Are they reaching for more sunlight to help you grow, or stretching aimlessly and exhausting your energy?

After a spell of depression during my sophomore year of college, I fixed a broken piano that sent me on an energizing musical journey. Funnily enough, I'd had a keyboard in my room that I'd bought a year prior, but

I hadn't spent much time playing it. I tapped into my inspiration in wonderful new ways as well as learned the need to manage its impact on my body.

MARCUS TALES #13
Off Beat

Midnight, two in the morning; it didn't matter. Nothing would stop me from playing my keyboard every night after fourteen-hour workdays instead of just doing my homework and going to sleep as I had been for months.

I made a point to practice the instrument and connect with the melodies humming inside of me. Many of these melodies were inspired by my experiences, emotions, and experimenting. I composed songs and shared them with others, looking for feedback.

Now, I attended a conservatory and was learning the instrument by ear. My classmates who attended the school for music were positioned to be leaders in their fields, and I was conscious that I had a fraction of their experience. I had some concern that they might make fun of me for not knowing the notes or how to read music, so I chose my audience carefully and shared nonetheless.

I felt incredible each time I shared. My friends gave me awesome feedback, driving me to practice with renewed energy. The late-night rehearsals were well worth the lost sleep.

I was eating in the dining hall when a friend whom I had not seen in a while said to me, "Hey, Marcus, great to see you! Are you okay, man? You're not looking too good."

"Oh yeah? What do you mean?" I asked him.

He told me I had some darkness around my eyes, so I went to the bathroom to look at myself. My friend had a point—I looked exhausted and weak and hadn't realized. The late nights were energizing my spirit, but my body paid the price. It became apparent that I'd stopped applying discipline to my time management; an incredible spiritual practice that grew from my inspiration turned into a vice.

I returned and thanked him for letting me know. He happened to be a music major so I invited him to come to my dorm and hear what I'd been up to, to learn the reason why I looked as ragged as I did. We had a great time, played music together, and he invited me to play with some friends of his.

Unfortunately, our schedules conflicted far more than they aligned and it was difficult to find a time to play. The three sessions we managed to organize started an avalanche of problems for me; I missed my first class out of weariness, couldn't participate in a crew activity later that week because of my exhaustion, and let down my new music friends. We'd planned to play together at an event and I had to pull out due to fatigue and needing to catch up on my responsibilities.

This experience taught me that inspiration can be a powerful tonic for the spirit, but we must balance the urges of the spirit with our well-being and community. While the music brought me out of a depression, it led me to neglect my body and compromise my balance. Our inspirations should enrich our community, but I let mine down when I missed the crew call and couldn't perform with the musicians.

All this occurred because I did not exercise control over my inspiration. I could have made sleep and the entirety of my well-being a priority and considered that there was virtually no way to fit music rehearsals into my already full schedule. I could have continued practicing in my room instead of trying to play with others, which pushed me to compromise both my inspiration and self in the process. Thankfully, I learned my lesson and now have a better understanding of how I can incorporate my inspirations into my routines without jeopardizing my mind, body, or relationships with others.

Compose Yourself with
Your Vibration

Did you know that plants are singing all the time? If you're unfamiliar with this phenomenon, know the songs are the results of vibrations. There are even devices we can connect to our plants that translate their vibrations into sounds we can hear. Unsurprisingly, every plant has a different song to share.

Everything is vibrating all the time because everything in the universe is moving, and these vibrations create patterns known as frequencies. Even if we cannot hear the songs of our plants with our ears alone, we are still sensitive to the frequencies they emit. We are affected by all frequencies emitted, and we affect others with ours.

Every part of us is vibrating and emitting a different frequency, and your state of being determines the vibration your being collectively emits. Imagine if your state of being was condensed into a song with its tempo representing the ebb and flow of your day. Would this be a happy, angry, or sad song? Now imagine that this song is played by an entire orchestra. The instruments may not be playing the same note or playing the same tempo, but they are playing in unison to create the song. You are the orchestra. Alive, the orchestra of your being is working and playing a song at every moment. This tune is your vibration, and it affects your community and environment.

Each of us has a vibration and we can control it with breathing, control, and composure. I use kindness to embrace these vibrations and frequencies, and to connect with others.

The same can be said about the vibration and frequency of our being. Spiritual harmony gives our being a calming and inviting vibration, and the frequency we emit is equally as peaceful. With consciousness of our vibration and frequency, we can bring our best selves forward. We can pay attention to the tone of our voice when we speak, our demeanor, and our attitude, and use them to improve the quality of our experiences. There is power in how we compose ourselves. Respect this power, and use it to forward your growth.

I noticed a couple of my plants looked thirsty one morning so I thought I'd water them. Upon picking up the watering can, which was nearly empty save a little bit of water sloshing around the bottom, I heard a little chirp. I stopped and listened . . . and heard it again! Inside the watering can was a bird who must have fallen in and had no way of getting free. I figured the little guy would be scared so I gently reached my hand inside.

Conscious that my hand is an extension of myself, I fixated on adapting my vibration to be welcoming, one that the bird would find nurturing. He hopped on my hand and I pulled him out. He was only a baby, just learning to fly. Over the course of the five minutes I held him in my hand, I concentrated on maintaining a soothing vibration, trying not to scare the bird any more than he already was. It worked, and as the minutes passed, the bird wrapped his little talons around my fingers and enjoyed the warmth I provided. If I had been nervous or jumpy, I would have frightened him.

As we grow alongside other plants and creatures in our garden, we need to practice managing our vibration. That way, we'll be prepared to adjust if those around us are negatively affected by the frequencies we emit, and we can adapt if we are impacted by theirs.

Stay Alert by Practicing Stillness

Things in our lives ebb and flow, and chaos ensues when there's more ebb than flow. With more social maintenance responsibilities such as phone calls, voice mails, text messages, emails, and so on, it's no wonder why we all feel a little frazzled every now and then. The bombardment of our notifications, along with pressure to perform and respond to the world around us, can make it hard to tune out and prioritize our well-being. If I feel myself losing my peace, balance, or harmony, I remind myself to practice *stillness*, the art of slowing down and centering myself to listen and observe.

I've learned a good deal about stillness from observing my plants. Unless they are occupied with a task, such as conserving energy, I believe they are alert and practicing stillness. I say this because of their adaptability. Plants must be deliberate in the directions they grow, feeling out the best places for their roots, vines, leaves, and flowers. Have you ever been in a room with people who are trying to solve a problem but won't stop talking over one another so they don't make any progress? I've been in this situation too many times, and it makes me think of two different pothos plants I have next to each other on a ledge under my bedroom ceiling.

Both these plants need sunlight to survive, and space up there is limited. They have grown in a fascinating fashion; they've filled the space between them with their leaf-covered vines in a way that has allowed both to thrive. They're not taking over the common space or covering the other's vines—they're sharing it. They grow well together and I think this is because they work slowly and calmly, listening to each other and staying alert. In their stillness, they are ready to adapt and accommodate each other while continuing to grow. I haven't needed to trim them as they found a compromise and made room for all their leaves.

Stillness promotes awareness. Let's try it for a moment: Close your eyes. Inhale as much as you can, then exhale as much air as you can. Not only is this a refreshing activity, but it will bring your breathing to your attention. Get into a rhythm of breathing that is comfortable to you, and let it bring you a sense of calmness. Use this calmness to focus on what you can hear externally. If your thoughts are too loud for you to hear what's going on around you, take another deep breath with a great exhale. When you find a sense of quiet clarity, listen again. What do you hear? Are other living beings near you? How are you affecting them, and how are they affecting you? Take a moment in your stillness to center yourself, increase your alertness, and realign your vibration with harmony.

We discussed the importance of slowing down to practice patience in Part I, but now I will share that it's more than just a means of maintaining my peace and positive mindset—it's also how I connect my vibration with the vibrations around me. This stillness puts me in a state of alertness that makes it easier for me to see cause and effect. I can use this awareness to be a conduit of positivity for my community and environment, putting energy and time where it will be the most useful.

Use Prayer and Meditation to Engage

The harmony that comes from peace and balance within us is a microcosm of the macrocosm of harmony that comes from our community and environment working together. That harmony is a microcosm of the macrocosm of harmony present in the solar system with stars, planets, and moons all orbiting one another. All these facets of existence are connected, and these connections can be suppressed or cultivated. Common practices to cultivate those relationships include forms of meditation and prayer. Asteroids, weather, and sickness happen, disrupting the harmony in the universe, planet, and our bodies. Rather than contribute to this chaos, we can support harmony through positivity.

Meditation and prayer vary around the world from culture to culture. Meditation generally focuses on the

Life inside us, realigning our vibrations and finding stillness while people use prayer to connect with the greater force of Life outside us. Nobody has the same approach to meditation and prayer, but I find that meditation serves as a great practice to connect with oneself and prayer as a means to communicate with the larger entity that is Life.

The short activity we used to practice stillness (see the last section, "Stay Alert by Practicing Stillness" as well as the breathing practice mentioned in Chapter 7) can serve as a meditation exercise if extended for at least ten minutes. It forces you to listen to yourself as well as what's going on around you. The better you perfect this skill, the easier it is to focus on your positive mindset, find a rhythm that supports your balance, and harness your harmony to preserve your well-being.

I use prayer to engage and communicate with Life. Somewhere in my childhood, I heard of a phrase: "The will of the universe." The concept struck me and I carried it with me, thinking, *If the universe has a will, I should do my best to work with the universe instead of against it.* I began speaking out to the universe at an early age to collaborate with its will. Years later, I continue to practice this and view it as a form of prayer.

Prayer takes many forms. I have experience in

praying with people who represent various religions and spiritual affiliations, learning from their methods and goals. My experiences taught me that those who practice engaging with the universe find that it engages back, regardless of what kind of prayer they are doing. If praying is new to you, embrace the opportunity to connect with something greater than yourself and reap the benefits. People use prayer to work through problems, find peace during times of uncertainty, share positivity with our collective spirit, and offer gratitude. This is not a comprehensive list of reasons to pray, and as always, I encourage you to experiment and find your own ways to wield this tool.

People ask me all the time if I speak to my plants, and if it's true that speaking to one's plants helps them grow. I do speak to my plants, but I will not say it's absolutely true that speaking to your plants helps them grow. I believe it depends on what one says, and what one's intentions are. We cannot forget the frequencies we send out when we speak and pray. Vibrations bounce and can return to us. If I tell my plants they are ugly and useless, I can't expect them to grow better. Doing so would also invite my own negativity to come back to me. In my garden, I say out loud to my plants, "I'm here to help you grow, and to learn about myself in the process." I believe I am projecting my intention to a force greater than myself, my plants, or my garden—that force being Life—potentially amplifying the effects of my goals and actions. My plants respond to the positivity in my words and demeanor with brighter colors, stronger forms, and by looking "happier."

Community

Bring Plants Together

We've learned how to use harmonious spiritual practices to elevate the condition of our spirit and increase our spiritual awareness. Roots in the ground, composed, alert, and engaged, now we can put our spiritual awareness into practice by acknowledging we're only one plant in a greater garden. Have you taken time to notice the other plants growing around you? Do you know the birds and bees who sniff at your petals, hoping to take a drink from your nectar? How do their frequencies affect you? Is the community of your garden helping you grow, or are you struggling to flower?

Practice and persistence are one part of starting a garden and fostering a healthy community, but another is embracing the connection to the land and those who share it with us. I am not the only being to enjoy my garden, nor do I want to be. Where some people use pesticides and other means of deterring creatures from their yards, I've tried to work with the different animals and insects who pay my garden a visit. I recognize that each one has the potential to contribute to the prosperity of the land in some way, and that I could not curate this space on my own. My goal is not to create a picture-perfect manicured aesthetic; I'm focused on fostering a space where life can grow.

What we're planted with and who visits our garden impacts our growth. If we're open to it, a quality community can empower us in ways we didn't know were possible. Pothos can grow healthy long leafy vines when isolated in a pot on its own; planted next to a tree, the roots, vines, and leaves of the same plant will grow more than tenfold in size. We can accomplish things together that are unattainable on our own, as we have the potential to be resources and tools for each other.

I believe spiritual awareness means respecting all forms of life. This means valuing connection among all people and creatures around us. Nurturing these connections fosters strong communities, communities with cohesion, cooperation, and collective growth. Quality community provides us with care, support, encouragement. Overlooking the responsibility to maintain our community ties can leave us isolated, burdened, and overwhelmed. I define community as a group of beings sharing energy, resources, and/or an environment, and I have observed two major forms of community in my lifetime: *Greater Communities* and *Chosen Communities*.

There are times when someone or something in our community, Greater or Chosen, stifles the growth of others and we need to address these connections for the betterment of everyone. Using kindness, patience, and positivity in our communication will help us have these difficult conversations productively as well as improve our communication in general.

There is harmony in communities that work together, the same way there is harmony within ourselves when the three parts of our being work together. Our vibration will harmonize with whatever vibration our community is putting out. A healthy community will resonate and encourage growth, but a destructive community will reverberate and disrupt harmony. The ability to maintain growth is tied to community, so knowing how we affect and are affected by our community is invaluable information for our spiritual awareness.

Find Different Ways to Connect: Greater Communities and Chosen Communities

We frequently think of community as something we share with people only. Spending time in my garden continuously shows me that community is something we share with everything that lives, not just people. In the springtime, my garden is filled with beautiful creatures. Birds perch on my oleander trees and sing to one another as they gather sticks to build nests. Squirrels, as troublesome as they can be, bury their treasures in my grass to come back to at a later time. Bees and butterflies fly from my roses to my petunias in their search for nectar.

The birds help me by regulating the worm population, and making sure it doesn't grow too large. The squirrels till the soil as they dig—I don't always understand why they choose where they do, but I know it's with intention. The bees and butterflies pollinate my plants and keep the ecosystem alive. As I pour energy into my plants, I provide for these creatures, and I am filled with joy when I watch them scamper and flutter through my garden. In return, these insects and animals do maintenance to my garden in ways that I can't.

Together, we create a productive and reciprocal community in the environment of my garden.

In our *Greater Community*, we are connected to every living thing in our environment. Every squirrel that sniffs at our fruit, snail that eats our leaves, and weed that grows in our soil is part of our Greater Community. I don't believe there are strict parameters to what defines the size of the environment that encompasses our Greater Communities. The parameters change with where we are. At home, my Greater Community is my house, front yard, and garden. At a beach, I'd say the environment of the Greater Community extends as far as I can see. The environment of the *Greater Community of Earth* is the entire planet.

I came to understand the concept of a Greater Community when my childhood town started building houses in a muck field where millions of rats and mice lived. When we took away their habitat, they needed a new place to live and came to live with us. They took advantage of the real estate in the Greater Community of the town. Scores of mice found their way into businesses and the homes of neighborhoods across town, rich and poor alike.

The rodents had never been a problem before the construction in the field. In their search for a new home, they brought all sorts of trouble. They ate so much of the town's food that restaurants had to close. I'd hear hundreds of them squeaking and pitter-pattering on the roof as I'd try to sleep at night. We set traps all over, and my mother would collect hundreds of caught rodents at a time. People used poison to deal with the rodents, and when the town's pets ate the poisoned creatures, the poison took them, too.

As bizarre and tragic as the experience was, it showed me how connected all living beings are because of the environment we share. We disrupted and displaced the rodents, prompting them to come to our side of town and change our way of living. I didn't hold this against the mice. Had we left the field as it had been, they would have had no reason to leave it. We humans often separate ourselves from other animals, but the truth is we're more intertwined with our animal siblings than we think.

Spiritual awareness is about respecting all forms of life and nurturing the connections between us, and this starts in our Greater Communities. Community is virtually unavoidable given that our Greater Communities are defined by where we are at any moment, and we are very rarely the only being in an environment. For the most balanced and prosperous garden, respect those you share space with, provide and receive support, and contribute to growth other than your own. Foster growth with your choices and actions, and encourage others to do the same.

Beyond our Greater Communities, we have our *Chosen Communities*: groups of people united by a common goal, interest, and/or characteristic who share a sense of fellowship. I am part of Chosen Communities that enrich my life, such as my network of friends and family in Texas or the monastery where I lived and studied. My athletic friend is part of a *capoeira* community in the Twin Cities, and my singer friend is part of the performing arts community in Chicago. Each of these friends also has a community of loved ones on top of their interest-based communities, all while participating in the Greater Community of their respective environments and the Greater Community of Earth.

In a word, my college years were busy. Free time was a luxury I rarely had. After years of social isolation, a trip inspired me to enrich my life by creating a Chosen Community with some friends during my senior year. The character improvement and mutual growth that ensued are a testament to the power of community.

MARCUS TALES #14
The Brotherhood

My course load in college kept me constantly occupied. I'd chosen this school because of its commitment to a high standard for theater production; we produced the highest levels of shows outside of what's seen on Broadway or in Las Vegas. It was rigorous, and students had to be invited back every year to continue pursuing their degree. It was common for students to wind up on probation or sent home.

With the onslaught of work that we had, there was not a lot of time to make connections with people outside of our program, year, or particular show we worked on. Between the dancers, singers, actors, musicians, and film students, we had shows and productions occurring all the time. Technicians run everything so we were among the busiest students on campus.

In the beginning of my junior year, three friends from my program and I took a trip to visit a friend's brother's fraternity house in another state. My school didn't have fraternities, and I'd never been to a fraternity house, so seeing sixteen fraternity brothers living in the same space sharing camaraderie was exciting to see. Growing up in an adopted family led me to understand "family" to be the people you surround yourself with, and the brothers seemed like a happy and genuinely connected family to me.

Embarking on the road trip with my friends was a blast. After spending time at the fraternity house, I realized my friends and I could benefit from having a similar type of community. I started thinking of some of the younger students in my program as well as people I'd been struck by in conversation and thought they might be interested, too.

"I think it would be wise for us to all meet up at the same time, outside of the workday," I told each of them.

"For what?" everyone asked me. I honestly didn't have a solid idea in mind, but having us all come together seemed like a good start.

At 12:00 a.m. one morning, thirteen of us met in someone's living room. The group of young men was made of sophomores, juniors, and seniors, mainly theater technicians with a couple film students. One by one, we shared who we are, our goals for the program, and what we hoped to accomplish in the future. Although we all knew one another, this was the first we'd ever sat down to truly learn about each other.

In just forty minutes of us spending time together, we were energized and invigorated. We could have continued talking and sharing until sunlight poured through the windows, but we had to wake up early and get back to the grind. We unanimously agreed to meet up the following week at the same time.

Over the course of the next several months, those of us who continued to meet regularly noticed an improvement in our well-being. I had an elevated mood and felt more resilient. With a community to lean on for support, consult in times of challenge, and celebrate with in times of accomplishment, I felt more balanced and at peace, yielding more harmony than I'd had in years prior. The other brothers in the group reported the same.

The effects of having this community were noticeable to others. People regularly commented on the positive changes they observed in us, telling us we were respectful, considerate, and thoughtful. One brother was inspired to resolve issues in his family.

"My son told me the difference in his temperament comes from these weekly meetings you're having. We are so thankful," his mother emotionally told me over the phone.

Community has a direct effect on how we act and how we grow. We want to surround ourselves with communities that reinforce stability, discipline, resilience, and direction. I'm thankful to have had this experience, and it motivates me to foster a community of a similar caliber everywhere I go.

Addressing Unhealthy Connections

Sometimes, we don't work well together. Maybe the frequency of another plant is toxic to our leaves, or a squirrel eats us faster than we can grow back. When this happens, a change may be necessary for the betterment of a community and those who share it.

Maintenance and observation are often the difference between the success and failure of a long-term connection. After a couple years of harmonious cohabitation, I had to address one of my plant experiments: canna bulbs added to a bed where elephant ears were planted. Elephant ears can grow up to seven feet tall, with broad leaves (hence the name) that can grow up to two feet wide and three feet long. Canna bulbs are plants with paddle-shaped leaves, and leafstalks in varying shades of color. Canna bulbs produce beautiful flowers and can grow up to six feet tall. When I first planted the canna bulbs, they had only grown a few inches, whereas the elephant ears were about three feet tall. I didn't anticipate their heights becoming a problem for several years.

This combination was inspired by a visual idea: I imagined that the oval paddle-shaped canna bulb leaves would look lovely growing out under the massive heart-shaped leaves of the elephant ears. For about two years this experiment appeared to be working beautifully until I noticed the elephant ears looked unhealthy. Both plants had grown considerably; by now, the elephant ears stood over six feet tall and the canna bulbs had spread out and were standing at around four feet. After close observation over two weeks, I knew that the elephant ears were dying. Given the elephant ears had been healthy in that location for the previous two years, I determined that the canna bulbs were the issue because their roots were stifling and strangling the roots of the elephant ears. I realized the canna bulbs needed to be removed immediately.

Despite my best efforts, these two plants could not survive together in this location. This reminded me that sometimes when we are paired with others, whether it be in a community, family, or a workplace, our partner doesn't always help us grow. If this is the case, despite the difficulty, we have to do our best to carefully uproot and relocate. It is important we nurture each other's roots and respect those we share our space with. Even if we disagree with those around us, it's important we always leave room to grow.

It's easy to become the canna bulbs in a group if we aren't conscious of how we share resources and space. We can stunt the growth of those we love or share space with through a simple lack of awareness of how our choices affect those around us. Realizing personal growth at the expense of our communities hinders the progress and potential of our communities. I saw this happen time and time again growing up.

Already crippled by discriminatory laws and policies, generational trauma, and in many cases, a life-threatening lack of resources, some people in my community sought wealth and status from thievery and violence. They might have experienced a short-term reward, but now, most of those who participated are dead and many others are incarcerated. Decades later, the community has a disruptive lack of men, older people do not have children to care for them, and the community is a fraction of the size it was. I often wonder what would have happened if everyone had decided to work together instead of fighting each other for personal gain.

When we focus on growing harmoniously, our communities prosper. Communication is a great way to make this happen.

Communicate Effectively: Apply Kindness, Patience, Positivity

I am not formally educated in botany nor do I consider myself a plant expert. When people learn I'm a self-taught gardener, they often ask if I've always had a green thumb. It's more apt to say that I have always had a passion for helping things grow. I believe my plants thrive for two main reasons: I have fostered a healthy community and environment for them, and I approach plant care with kindness, patience, and positivity.

Every time we repot a snake plant, water an orchid, or talk to our bonsai tree, we are communicating with our plants and they will respond accordingly. I've observed that my plants are healthiest when I handle them with kindness, apply patience in my process, and keep positivity in my outlook. This keeps me gentle, calm, and solution-oriented.

Likewise, to foster growth in our communities, we must communicate deliberately because communication is the foundation of community. I believe everything I do communicates something to others, and I want to say or show that I am willing to contribute to our collective progress. I've come to see that people are not too different from plants; to nurture community, I communicate with kindness, patience, and positivity.

The seeds we plant in our mind are the actions, gestures, and thoughts we nurture in our community. I want my interactions with my community to reflect my positive mindset and commitment to growth. Temperament and attitude matter. I find that others are more receptive to what I have to say when I put kindness in my voice and bring a smile to every situation. Kindness doesn't mean acting passively, ignoring problems and emotions, living in delusion, or accepting abuse; it means being present and considering our actions and attitude, and how they will help or hurt a situation. I use it to avoid bringing anger and frustration from one situation to another.

Acting before we have fully assessed a situation can exacerbate a problem or create new ones to address. Patience is key to productive communication because it allows us to slow down, think, and see the nuances in the situation before we act. Solving a problem takes precious energy and resources; applying patience ensures we use both wisely.

Our positive mindset guides our communication. I am positive when I communicate because exercising kindness and patience can be challenging to maintain, but I don't want to give up on either and create more problems for myself. With positivity, I am prepared to learn lessons. Every instance of productive communication and misunderstanding alike are opportunities to learn and improve as a communicator. Approaching any interaction with negativity will contribute to the deterioration of connections, and ultimately our community.

To improve our communities and better understand our trajectory for growth, we must learn about our environments.

Environment

Share the Same Soil

t's one thing to know *who* you're planted with—it's another to consider *where* you're planted. How long are the days in your garden? What kind of soil are you planted in? Are there trees that provide shade? Can you bloom year-round, or must you retreat to the ground when it's cold, waiting for spring's warmth to awaken you? We need to connect with the community that we share space and resources with, yet it's equally as important to know one's environment: the space we occupy and the resources that come with it.

I consider community and environment the two pillars of growth because of their eternal impacts on our growth and well-being, as well as on each other. The relationship between community and environment is as deep as the relationship between our mind and body. Environment gives space for a community to live, and the community must nurture the environment for both their health and longevity.

We are blessed to live on such a beautiful and complex planet, admiring its wonders and appreciating its gifts. Yet our connection to this combination of land and water, mountain peaks and whirlpools, is deeper than our residency. We, people, are made of the same elements that Earth is made of: fire, water, earth, and air. Earth is our main environment, and we share it with every single other being that is alive: the Greater Community of Earth.

Within this magical environment are the smaller regions where we live and spend our time. Our environments change with our location, much like our Greater Communities. Think of your environment similarly: Other than the Greater Environment of Earth, you have a *Greater Environment* that follows your every step. We also have *Chosen Environments*, or our place of residency be it a house, car, or jungle.

Regardless of where we are, if we're settled, or if we're nomadic, we need to know our environment. Environments directly influence our peace and balance, and therefore our ability to sustain harmony and a spiritual well-being. Using our spiritual awareness, we can make sure we are working *with* our environment and supporting its continued growth. It's in our best interest to respect and take care of the resources our environments provide us, and learn to adapt with the changes of our environments instead of trying to alter them for our own desires.

Don't Waste; Fertilize!

My growing collection of houseplants gives me quite a bit of work to do. I have to monitor their soil, keep them hydrated, and inspect them for signs of growth as well as decline. As I make my rounds, I inevitably collect a pile of dead leaves I pull from my pots and planters. Sometimes I'll leave a few dead leaves in the soil of the plants to nurture the soil, but I generally add them to my compost to feed my outdoor plants. If the plant is healthy, dead leaves aren't a concern of mine. They're a valuable resource I can combine with food scraps to create fertilizer for my garden.

With an activated spiritual awareness, we can see that opportunity exists everywhere and in every moment. Apply this to your environment, and you'll begin to notice how you can use it to maximize its potential and support yours in turn. What are the resources in your house? I always have a large bag of jasmine rice on hand because I cook rice often. I rinse my rice before I cook it and I'm sure to collect the "rice water" in a bowl for a couple reasons: I can use it to water my plants, and to pour over my hair for a boost of nutrition. Instead of wasting part of the resource of the rice by pouring its water down the drain, I use it to its full potential and to bolster my own. Healthy hair, healthy plants, healthy me!

Not using the rice water to better my hair could cost me resources in the future when my hair feels weak and I need to help it. It's easy to ask, *Why does this resource matter to me now?* I think a better question, considering that resources are finite, is, *How can I best use this resource now?* There's no guarantee all resources will be available when we need them, so finding use for them when we have them is the best way to respect our environment and foster harmony within it. Harmony in our environment will promote harmony within ourselves, supporting our spiritual well-being and growth.

Let harmony flow between you and your environment. After all, we're made of the same elemental building blocks: fire, water, earth, and air. Wasting the potential of your resources and your environment is to waste your own potential to grow. Using your resources to improve the quality of your environment or wellness will help you grow and nurture your environment, creating a wonderful cycle of continued success. I think of this when I sprinkle compost around my yard.

Using compost changed my environment for the better and completely reshaped how I approach fertilizer and waste. I started small with a five-gallon bucket for my food scraps and grew my system to multiple containers fit for different stages of the decomposition process. After some time (and practice), I had fertilizer to use so I got to work. I was astounded by the effect of the compost on my plants; it was like I'd given them steroids! Growth skyrocketed, flowers bloomed, and everything radiated with health. As the environment of my garden enjoyed the results of my repurposed resources, I, too, felt myself rejuvenated. I had more aloe vera to use, healthier grass to walk on, and a sense of accomplishment.

Everything in an environment is connected, every resource, every member of the community that inhabits it. Use your spiritual awareness to see these relationships, utilize your resources, and foster an environment where everything grows in harmony.

Adapt to Grow

I had so much to learn when I drove those sixteen houseplants to my new home in Texas from Florida.

It's hard to believe how little I understood about the complexities of plant care back then, but I'm happy to share that I've come a long way. Losing half those plants sparked my journey in gardening and I still ache to think of the ones I lost. To make sure I don't make those same mistakes again, I've spent time thinking about what went wrong all those years ago.

Years later, I now understand the importance of environment. The Houston area is considered subtropical while central Florida is tropical. I didn't know I needed to or how to help my plants acclimate to the different conditions of their new environment. My "plant mom," the Floridian woman who gave me these plants, offered me tips but I didn't understand how to use the wisdom she shared. Thankfully she continues to treat me with wonders from her plant collection, and I've learned to use my reasoning to help them adapt and keep growing.

I didn't change my house to fit the needs of the plants after I lost the first set. Instead, I did some research, observation, and thinking until I found places in my house that satisfied the conditions of each plant. This process reinforced something I'd long observed: our best chance of growth lies in adapting to and growing *with* our environments instead of *changing* our environments to fit our needs and desires.

Hundreds of plants now happily live in my house.

Imagine I find a stunning new plant with unique needs and choose to bring it home, only to learn the environment of my house cannot support it. I have two options: help the plant adapt over time, or modify my house to become more like its ideal environment. Changing the environment of my house to help this single plant could help it grow, but not without potentially jeopardizing the other plants that already adapted to this environment. Hundreds of unwell or dying plants—think of how much work this would give me! Patiently working with the plant, however, to find a place where it could grow would fold it into the current environment without disrupting the preexisting balance.

There are times when we may need to adjust our environments for the betterment of its own preservation along with the community it supports. In this case, we must remember to be respectful to its longevity and the community we share it with. This is especially prevalent to our Greater Environments and the Greater Environment of Earth. Check in with your Greater Community before enforcing any changes because every change we implement, from chopping down trees to building new structures, affects everyone involved. And, if we go to an environment and begin to prosper, we should make certain we are not growing at the expense of our community or environment.

I had a chance to slow my pace and grow in new ways when I spent some time at a monastery on beautiful lands with cherished gardens and lively woods. I would find places to write where I could enjoy the wonders of the space. When a monk expressed frustration for the state of his beloved rosebush, I realized my growth impacted my environment in ways I did not anticipate.

MARCUS TALES #15

Connecting with Deer

Around 2 a.m., underneath a bright moon shining high in the sky, I often sat between the massive roots of an oak tree, in a seat of earth that seemed to be created especially for me.

I would engage in reading, writing, and drawing. The moon is my friend and frequently illuminated the darkness for me so I didn't worry if I forgot a lamp. Other times, the lack of light from a lamp or the moon let me sit in complete darkness and contemplate.

There were several early mornings when I heard the soft padding of deer around me and could see them in the distance. Over time, I noticed they moved closer toward me and I suspected they were getting used to my scent. A deer locked eyes with me one early morning, and I did my best to calm my heartbeat and still myself so I would not scare the animal.

It was bold enough to come toward me. I did not pet it or reach out, and we sat in each other's presence for some time. I had some food with me and I placed it on the ground to share. The deer appeared to enjoy the snack, stood up, and went on its way.

I began bringing food with me on my walks along the grounds in the case any deer wanted some. In doing so, I developed great friendships with them. They felt more comfortable with me each day and moved close enough to let me pet them. I still think of how soft their fur felt. A deer surprised me one night when she nudged another deer, who seemed rather young to me, toward me. It was a mother presenting her baby to me! Touched, I continued embracing my new friends only to discover this community had caused some issues in our shared environment.

"The deer have been eating our roses again! Although we did some work to mitigate this situation, something seems to have brought them back."

My midnight snacks must not have been enough for my deer, and I imagine they followed my scent from the woods to the gardens. I had not known they had been a problem for the monks and that the monks had worked hard to get and keep them away. I was a guest at the monastery and it was not my space to change.

Although I was connecting with myself and the Greater Community of the monastery, my growth disrupted the operations of the monks and their environment. The gardens are not just for beauty—they are home to precious herbs needed for the wellness and traditions of the monks. I had no idea the deer would take our nightly rendezvous as an invitation to follow my scent and visit other parts of the grounds. My scent was all over!

I did not blame the deer. Had I known the deer were not to visit the gardens, I would have interacted with them differently. I grew, but at the cost of the monastery time and a few plants. I now seriously consider the impacts of my relationships and am sure to check in with my community before I do something that I think could affect our shared environment.

16

Collective Balance

Appreciate Everyone's Contribution

Years of learning, experimenting, practicing, and observing have led me to foster a lively environment where hundreds of different plants can grow together. My backyard garden is an oasis in my neighborhood, where animals and insects flock for food, sanctuary, and community. I watch proudly as anoles climb my pineapple plants, birds bathe in puddles after a storm, dragonflies perch on my trellis, and butterflies drink nectar from my marigolds. My small plot of land is full of life, and I am energized every time I step outside to embrace the community I've encouraged in our shared environment.

Every creature has a role in the community and environment of my garden. We have roles in ours, too. To promote success in the spaces we occupy and the beings we share them with, let's consider our impact and respect the contributions of others. Doing so will allow us to reach *collective balance*, a state of harmony resulting from every creature contributing to the continued success of the community and environment.

Various Roles: Consider Your Impact

I create two types of compost. One is made of organic matter such as vegetables, fruits, and plant cuttings, and the other is made exclusively of citrus. I'd learned that I could line plant beds with orange peels to create a boundary that would keep certain insects out of the plant beds and encourage others to stay inside. I thought to myself—why not try this with compost? I spent a year curating citrus compost so I could use it for this purpose, unaware that this idea would turn into a disastrous experiment for the community and environment of my garden.

When the time came, I scattered some of this compost around my yard and kept the majority of it in a compost bin on the ground. A little while later, something strange caught my eye as I churned the bucket. Something *moved*. I looked closer and found that grub worms and beetle worm larvae filled the bucket! I scanned my yard and saw the larvae had migrated and burrowed into the ground, killing some of my grass, plants, and part of a tree.

We all have a role in our community, and we choose how to contribute. These beetles are great at decomposing matter that other creatures avoid, and I celebrated their part in that process. Their role turned detrimental when they left the compost and began eating other plants in my garden. There's a lesson here: we can begin contributing to our community and environment positively, but without spiritual awareness of our impact in the long term, our contribution can turn harmful.

Every community and environment requires different roles to operate, and each is unique in what's needed. Roles evolve and change with time, too. For collective balance, we must use our spiritual awareness to remain conscious of our impact, fill the roles that are necessary, and prepare to adapt our roles over time. Collective balance takes collective effort, so communicate with others and find out what's needed in your community, and how you can maintain or adapt your role accordingly.

People seem to struggle to maintain collective balance more than our plants do. Why is working together a consistent challenge for us in our Chosen Communities and Chosen Environments? I think it's because people lose their composure, stop being alert, and disengage from their community or environment for self-preservation. We can mitigate this problem through improving our spiritual awareness, looking beyond ourselves, and prioritizing harmony.

Respect the Different Roles

We cannot achieve collective balance without respect: gratitude and admiration for the contributions and impact of others. We don't always get to choose what's planted near us and what it brings to the garden of our community or how it changes our environment. We may feel reluctant to let another plant's roots grow closer to where we've been happily growing, but community is an opportunity. Even if we don't like the smell of another flower or the pesky aphids who feed on its fruit, we should withhold judgment and respect what this single plant can offer to the shared environment.

I was surprised by an unlikely and unintentional pairing one autumn. My pomegranate tree served as the perfect trellis for my cucumber vine when it began to grow rapidly, seeking something to climb and buttress its growth. The tree branches supported the vegetable plant as it grew from its roots in the ground to the top of the tree, nine feet high, and it produced the largest cucumbers I'd ever seen! I didn't have to prune my pomegranate tree the way I had in years prior because the weight of the cucumbers on the vines actually pulled the pomegranate branchlets apart enough so that new ones could grow out of the ground. I didn't foresee this when I planted the cucumber in the corner of my garden. Both plants experienced a healthy growing season, and I smiled to see the harmony between them.

We may surprise ourselves with whom and where we find community. We may not realize what resource we can be for others, and how they may support our growth in turn. We can be like the pomegranate tree and cucumber plants in our own relationships and grow together. Fighting for resources with those we share space with instead of working together is detrimental for all. We're likely to waste resources as we recover from our battle, and lose time to unnecessary recuperation that sets us behind in our growth.

I should note an important caveat: respect is earned. We cannot expect our community to share resources with us and be willing to work together unless we show that we are prepared to show the same respect. If you go to a new environment and join a new community, use your spiritual awareness to consider the needs of others. Make sure your desires and goals don't disrespect others and stunt their growth, and communicate if theirs affect you.

Opportunity is everywhere, and so is the potential for collective balance. Offer your branch, and it might be exactly what you and a vine need. I learned this when a friend helped me battle some squirrels and changed my life in unanticipated ways. I didn't realize how the role of her friendship would impact my future but quickly came to respect it.

MARCUS TALES #16
Garden Help

I walked into my garden one morning to see the strawberry plant I'd been caring for finally produced a berry ripe enough for me to eat. I left for work, excited to return home and try my homegrown fruit. I usually finished work after sundown, but it was daylight when I made it home.

I opened the gate and walked around the corner, spotting a flash of brown in the corner of my eye. A squirrel had been inside my planter with the strawberry plant. . . . It flew out of the pot and ran up my Arizona ash tree, knocking over my strawberry plant in the process. High in the tree, it made eye contact with me. In its thieving little hands was the strawberry I'd waited all day to eat. It continued to look at me while it ate before throwing the stem onto the ground like it was nothing.

The furry bandits had been digging in my planters and destroying my garden for months, and this final act marked the start of a war. Wasting no time, I prepared for battle. I researched, experimented, and tried various methods to keep the rodents away from my plants. They kept advancing and eating whatever they could.

I finally thought of buying a mesh material that has a texture I heard squirrels don't like. I planted my plants in the ground, put soil on top, added a layer of the mesh, and covered it with a sprinkle of soil and some mulch. My thought was that the squirrels would dig through the mulch only to meet the fabric and be deterred from digging further.

I tried the experiment, and it worked! I was thrilled to think I could win the next series of battles. The only problem was the time it took to plant the fabric. I'd been telling a new friend about my war with the squirrels, and she offered to come over and help me plant the mesh. Together, we tackled my largest plant bed—a ring of caladiums and purple queen surrounding my Arizona ash tree.

We had a great conversation while we worked, and she helped me in more ways than one. Our time together rekindled my relationship between myself and my inspiration. I shared the *Tool Versus Vice* dichotomy (see Introduction) with her, and she perked up with questions to ask about the concept. For the first time in years, I dusted off my old notebooks.

Going through my old notebooks had once brought me peace, clarity, and inspiration. Until she came over, I hadn't realized I'd become removed from a quality community and that work had increasingly consumed my days. I'd stopped making time to write down my reflections and have conversations centered around my growth. I felt more energized with each page turn.

My friend shared with me that our friendship fostered positive change in her life as well, leading to a new exploration of her inspiration, improvement in her well-being, and a peace she'd never experienced.

After I shared my writing with my friend, she asked me if I'd ever considered sharing my thoughts and observations on a larger scale. Years later, this friend is now the cofounder of my company and my creative partner.

I continue to respect those in my community and the potential role they may play in my future.

In Sum

We often fail to acknowledge the importance of a healthy spirit in our modern age and focus instead on a robust mental health and physical fitness. That does not change the fact that our well-being is incomplete without a strong spirit and spiritual awareness.

Our spirit is our connection to everything that lives outside of ourselves. Cherish this connection, and if you feel yourself losing it, return to your spiritual practices. I suggest doing a spiritual practice at least twice a week. You may enjoy making an occasion out of it—setting up a space where you feel comfortable, turning off and putting away your devices, and immersing yourself in the experience.

Increase your composure and alertness, and practice engaging with Life to hone your spiritual awareness. Every choice we make impacts our community and environment just as we are affected by where we are and who is around us, and our spiritual awareness is vital to seeing these patterns. A much overlooked aspect of gardening is managing the relationships that exist within a garden. Think of yourself as a gardener of your own community and environment, and use your spiritual awareness to help them prosper.

Peace in your mind, balance in your body, and harmony in your spirit are the ingredients for continued growth and resilience. Sustaining collective balance takes contribution from all community members and a respect for the shared environment. It's more than possible to achieve such a harmony, but it takes motivated people who are committed to self-improvement. Each of us is a member of a community tasked with managing our own harmony so we can fit into the symphony of Life around us.

It's no small task, but we can take small steps to get there. Let's start by focusing on ourselves, our vibration, and the frequency we emit. When we feel confident in our harmony, let's connect with our communities and share our elevated spiritual state with them, and encourage harmony between us. We can grow together, but we have to choose to.

Propagate a Pineapple and
Use Your Resources

In this activity, we'll turn food scraps into plants and re-mind ourselves that we often have more resources than we realize.

1. Acquire a healthy pineapple, chef's knife, cutting board, and an eight-ounce glass jar/cup filled with water.

2. Cut the crown off the pineapple. Some people prefer to twist off the crown, but I prefer to cut.

3. Set aside the fruit to enjoy later.

4. Pull off the bottom two to three inches of leaves from the crown and add them to your compost (or discard).

5. Place the crown in the jar of water. The leaves should be above the jar with only the leafless part of the crown submerged.

6. Watch over the next few weeks as roots grow! Don't worry if your crown turns brown; as long as the roots are growing, this pineapple is still alive and growing.

7. When your crown has grown two to three inches of roots, it's ready for soil. Get a six-inch planter filled with soil if you are not planting directly in the ground, and gently plant the roots and leafless bottom of the crown in the soil. The leafy part of the crown should rest above the soil.

8. Nice work—you have just planted a pineapple plant that will continue growing with care and potentially produce fruit someday! What may have gone into your compost or trash is now a lovely plant. Be creative with your resources— they may have more purpose than you think!

Note: Propagating food like pineapples, lettuce, onions, carrots, and potatoes is a great way to cheaply grow your own food, minimize food waste, and add to your plant collection. I currently have seven pineapple plants growing in my yard and although it could be years before any of them produce fruit, I love the look of their spiky leaves and knowing that I turned one pineapple into an entirely new plant.

Conclusion

t's never too late to focus on our growth, and it's never too soon to start.

The lessons I've drawn from my experiences and the tools I've collected have helped me overcome adversity great and small, find light in darkness, and foster community in unlikely places. I sharpen and clean my tools regularly for continued use, wield them with intention, and look out for new ones to aid me on my way. I look forward to the next chapters of my life and hope you do, too.

The lessons I have learned in the garden were never ones I planned to share widely, but when I started posting videos from my garden showing what we can learn from plants, people responded. The drive to nurture and grow exists in all of us, but the choice to begin the journey is yours.

We have learned how to harness our mental health, physical fitness, and spiritual awareness. We're ready to face our experiences with ingenuity and resilience. Bringing the mind, body, and spirit together will help you unlock your potential, find peace, develop balance, and sustain harmony. Now, I will share key barriers to growth I've confronted in myself as well as observed in others and how to move past them.

Let's increase our potential for growth by considering our motivation, our priorities, and our focus. We can eliminate unnecessary pressure by remembering we have nothing to prove, and focus instead on a lifetime of learning and the joys that follow.

A Motivation to Learn

In the six years since I bought my house, I've grown my garden and plant collection from a few exotic houseplants to a space where green is everywhere I look. The fence that demarcates my backyard is lined with plant beds full of purple queen, sweet potato ivy, lilies, ferns, banana trees, elephant ears, palms, canna bulbs, and hibiscus flowers. Plants hang from my fence, trees, and house, and my back porch is covered in pots and planters. With greenery overflowing on every cabinet, table, windowsill, and shelf, I've started hanging plants from my ceiling, walls, and curtain rods.

I began with a handful of houseplants and a determination to learn. Every time my experiments failed or I lost a plant, I chose to learn *how* and *why*. I could have given up after losing my first nine plants or my fifteenth experiment gone awry, but I knew I'd never improve as a gardener if I did. I might be blessed with a passion for helping things grow, but my knowledge and understanding has come from years of continued practice and a determination to learn.

The same motivation that pushed me to confront adversity throughout my life drove me to become a better gardener. I saw my determination to grow in my plants, and the mysteries of plant care began to unravel. Growth does not need to be complicated. Instead we should think of growth as incremental, done over time.

Each of us begins our journey in different parts of the rosebush. I was born into the thorns, but I now spend my days among the colorful flowers and their fragrant petals. Callouses from pricks I experienced in times past remain and are agitated from time to time, but I'm working to remove them with patience and determination. The process has proved exhausting and laborious, yet it's what I've needed to do to improve my well-being. My reward is my motivation: a brighter future and a better self. I'm not finished growing. And neither are you.

Regardless of where you started, where you are, what you've dealt with, and what you're facing, you too, can grow. You only need to find the motivation.

Value Versus Worth

If I bring home an orchid that has yet to flower with the sole goal of seeing it flower, I'm likely to overwater it in my hopes of helping it grow, or underwater it because I don't care about the process needed to yield a reward. Either way, I'll probably kill or stunt the plant.

I have seen people focus more on work and money than their minds, bodies, and spirits. They waste unparalleled talent and artistry, the type we are fortunate to see once in a generation, because they won't slow down to take care of themselves or respect their relationships with others. When this happens, we're falling into the trap of confusing *Value* and *Worth*. I define *value* as "the amount of money, property, and/or assets one has," and *worth* as "the measure of one's mental health, physical fitness, and spiritual awareness (or the state of one's well-being)." We should prioritize worth over value because without worth, our lives are doomed to chaos.

I imagine there was a time when people could cultivate and balance their worth and value with their own motivation, but we replaced motivation with incentive somewhere along our way. I use the dichotomy of *Incentive Versus Motivation* to think about where my drive comes from as I approach my responsibilities, hobbies, habits, and routines. Our time is limited, and we need value to survive in a world that favors it over the well-being of people. I find that incentive is tied to value the way motivation is tied to worth. But what happens when we forget how to access our motivation?

If we become accustomed to working for incentive, it may be harder for us to accomplish goals out of motivation. We may struggle to find purpose in tasks if we cannot see a short-term reward. Long-term endeavors, such as a healthy well-being, can then appear fruitless and not worth the effort. Losing our motivation primes us to chase value at the cost of our worth, jeopardizing our well-being and stunting our growth and the growth of others.

A quality well-being is priceless. A positive mindset, understanding of one's body, and a connection to

Life equip one for limitless growth and all the joy that accompanies it. If we commit to a quality well-being, our work is never finished. We spend our lifetimes patiently nurturing and tending to ourselves, and the reward is our wellness. Our well-being is our own responsibility and therefore we are self-motivated, driven to live a more fulfilling life. Value, in contrast, is generally not self-driven the way motivation is. We complete tasks and responsibilities for the promise of a tangible reward—income.

We must support every stage of an orchid's growth to see its flower, just as we need to care for our well-being in order to grow. Among the people I've watched waste unique skills and artistic talent were good friends of mine, but their focus on value strained my commitment to worth. I had to leave them because I never lost my motivation to grow. I knew it was time to go when their choices began affecting my ability to sustain my mental health, physical fitness, and spiritual awareness. Had I lost my focus, I might have continued down their path.

Maintain Your Focus

To seek growth, prioritize worth, and stay motivated, we need focus. Be sure to assess challenges along the way, or goals you have—but be careful not to mistake this for judgment. We don't want to be shortsighted or premature in our evaluation of ourselves: our inspiration, needs, and understanding of our hobbies, habits, and routines. If we disrupt our focus with distractions, we're likely to make judgments so we don't have to keep thinking about ourselves earnestly. Regularly questioning our hobbies, habits, and routines means we are assessing our choices and are prepared to adapt to changes. A habit that contributes to our growth could imperil it months later, but we would not know if we had judged the habit as absolutely beneficial to us.

My sweet potato ivy thrives during the summer and hibernates beneath the soil in winter. To nurture its growth during the warm season, I make sure it's watered every few days. In autumn, the plant begins its slow retreat into the ground. I water it weekly or biweekly because it needs less as the temperatures cool. If I made a judgment that the sweet potato ivy always needed the same amount of water, it wouldn't survive. Instead, I make assessments and adapt my care as needed. We are the same way. Even if we find a great combination of hobbies, habits, and routines, we cannot forget to assess our progress and question our choices because we exist in a state of constant change, along with our communities and environments. Judgments stem from a lack of focus.

We have other tools at our disposal to help us maintain focus on our well-being, too. Community is a powerful one. Other people can help us evaluate ourselves with clarity and objectivity. Trusted friends, mentors, and loved ones can see us in ways we cannot see ourselves, and their insight is invaluable to our success. Former students of mine still thank me for moments of clarity I gave them when academics, extracurriculars, and general adolescence distracted their focus from their well-being. I'm grateful to have been there for them when they needed it—not only because I could help them, but because a few of them started looking out for me, too.

We can be gardeners for our communities and encourage each other to have high standards for ourselves.

Standard Versus Expectation

An essential part of maintaining our well-being and bolstering our growth is committing to a standard. A *standard* is a level of quality, and I believe we should hold ourselves to high standards to maximize our potential. I have a standard for my behavior, my work, my company, the entertainment I consume, and so on. There's a standard for everything I can control in my life. Yet don't confuse this with expectations: we hinder ourselves when we replace standard with *expectation*, the belief that something is certain to happen or be in the future.

So live by a high standard and let go of expectations. There are no guarantees for the future so it's unproductive to act as if there are, and too many factors are outside of my control for my expectations to be realistic. Before I understood the difference between standard and expectation, I found myself frequently disappointed when situations did not play out as I'd hoped. Instead of resigning myself to a life at the whim of happenstance, I learned to live by a standard.

I am not trying to get any of my plants to look like any of the pictures online or in magazines, I am merely aiming to help them grow and learn in the process. This has yielded the best results as I don't put pressure on myself or on my plants.

Committing to a standard requires discipline while expectations rely on wishful thinking. Achieving a sound mental health, physical fitness, and spiritual awareness takes effort, so expecting a quality well-being without working for it will leave us frustrated and without progress. Everyone can benefit from a standard, regardless of our value, background, or what we look like. Having a standard means making the most of the resources at our disposal, doing our best and learning from our effort, and focusing on process rather than result.

Standard is individualized. Although we should aim for high standards, we can't force our standards onto others. The moment we ask someone to meet our standard, we are holding them to an expectation. We can only control what we do, not the actions of other people. We're also likely to be disappointed if we expect someone to meet our standard and the person fails to. Instead of judging or condemning others, I simply acknowledge when someone's standard is different than mine, and perhaps have a conversation about it.

I generally discourage people from concerning themselves with the expectations of others, but at times it's unavoidable. This is especially prevalent in the workplace. Other people, especially those in positions of power and authority, may project expectations onto us and leave us feeling pressured to perform or act according to their ideal. We can still apply our dichotomy and prioritize a standard. Ignoring expectations and aiming for a high standard means we will complete a task thoroughly and to the best of our ability. It removes external pressure and replaces it with self-motivation.

Operating this way has me routinely surpassing the expectations of others because I've practiced holding myself to a standard for years. If our standard consistently does not meet the expectations of people we're working with, we should communicate. We should try understanding why and where our standards differ and pursue a compromise.

I appreciate standards because they dissuade people from trying to *prove something*, another common obstacle to growth and self-improvement.

You Have Nothing to Prove on Your Journey

There is a purity in the growth of plants because they cannot stunt their own growth. A plant's decline results from its conditions, not a lack of will: the weather isn't right, the soil doesn't work, or a squirrel needs something to eat. People, however, can disrupt our growth in more ways than we can count, and having something to prove is no exception.

A common problem I saw in my students that I've seen in people everywhere is the desire to prove something to others. Maybe we want people to think we're funny or clever so we try to contribute to a conversation when we have nothing to say, and make a fool of ourselves in the process. Perhaps we think people will see us as incapable if we accept help instead of accomplishing a task on our own, even when we could benefit from some insight. So we try on our own, making unnecessary mistakes along the way. The folly of trying to prove oneself to others takes many forms, but it's always a distraction because it jeopardizes our focus, and therefore our peace, balance, and harmony. I find that we are more likely to achieve progress in our growth and well-being when we are driven by self-motivation rather than the ways others perceive us.

It's superficial to make choices for the sake of proving ourselves to others, and superficiality is shallow. We have depth and layers to our well-being and we need to nurture all of them. To act superficially is to touch only the surface of what others see rather than all of what there is to our mind, body, and spirit. Being the best person we can be speaks for itself.

We can take notes from our plants and remember that our caladiums do not try to be like elephant ears nor elephant ears like caladiums. They simply grow in their own way, at their own pace.

With nothing to prove, I've managed to keep my focus on learning and growing in everything I do. I don't let the pressures of others prompt me to move faster than I can because I know growth takes time.

Don't Rush

It's exciting to embark on a journey of self-improvement, peace, and balance, especially if one hasn't done it before. New beginnings are opportunities to reimagine the direction of our life and how we will steer it. The hopefulness we experience as we take our first steps is invigorating, and rightly so.

I see a similar ethos embodied in people who bring their first plant home, eager to give it everything it needs to grow and prosper. Our enthusiasm can lead us to harm the plant with our good intentions, though. I've referenced sweet potato ivy frequently throughout this work because so many of my early experiments involved this plant. One in particular taught me the importance of letting a plant be until it needs something. The garden expert at the store I bought it from suggested I plant it in a larger pot at home to give its roots space to grow. I did just that, and it grew considerably over the next two weeks. I thought it was time to repot it again to make space for its roots, so I planted it in a much larger planter. It wasn't ready for that size of planter and its growth stagnated.

The experience reaffirmed the necessity of pacing ourselves to sustain the momentum of our growth. As we incorporate new hobbies, habits, and routines into our lives, we must remind ourselves to slow down, and that there's no need to rush. Seeds do not grow into trees that produce fruit overnight; they take years, even decades. I encourage starting your new hobbies, habits, and routines at a pace that is realistic for your abilities and current responsibilities.

Meditating, for example, is a great practice to find mental peace and a tool I've used for years. Experienced meditators can measure their sessions in hours, while the majority of beginners will start with minutes. Over time, they can increase their endurance and lengthen their sessions with practice and persistence, but trying to meditate for an hour on one's first attempt could do more damage than good. Feeling overwhelmed or unsure of what to do might deter someone from meditating ever again.

If I had a plant for every time I told a student of mine to slow down, I'd have enough plants to fill my garden ten times over. My grandmother shared a mantra with me that I think of every day because I believe my plants are already embodying this: *Be a labor big or small, do it well or not at all. Once a task has begun, do it well until it's done.* I embraced these words fully. As I attempted to put them into practice, I noticed I only did so successfully when I started a task with a rhythm I could keep. Rushing created problems for me; I'd break material

I worked with, make mistakes I'd have to spend time rectifying, and frustrate myself to no end. Your growth is a great labor, one that will take you your life to complete. To do it well and until it's done, remember to *pace yourself*.

Growth: The Choice Is Yours

Choosing to begin an adventure of growth is a major step forward for your well-being, and I applaud all who make the choice. Addressing our mind, body, and spirit is a great undertaking with no shortage of hurdles and hiccups.

I started prioritizing my growth because my only other choice was to let my circumstances pull me down like a sinkhole in a garden. Perhaps you feel similarly.

Not everyone will support your endeavor toward growth. Some people are intimidated by those who commit to improving their well-being. Some simply see no value in such a journey without the incentive of a reward. Others are disconnected from what it means to grow, and from their position of stagnation they cannot imagine what it means to pursue and achieve personal development.

I have some advice for those who are met with

confusion or even resentment on their journey. First, listen to what people tell you because we should not be so arrogant as to dismiss the input of others. You can choose what you do with the information they share with you, but it's worth hearing people out, especially if they have your best interests in mind. Then, question your motivation. Are you pursuing growth for the sake of some incentive, or to be a more positive and productive person? If your motivation is rooted in improving your worth, and will not compromise your well-being, community, or environment, then be courageous. Carve a path forward for yourself. Be the person to start the garden. Some may follow and join you; others won't. It might feel lonely in the garden, but I've found it's better to be alone and growing than part of a toxic and stifling community. If you get discouraged, remember that your growth will foster and support new growth to follow.

We Cannot *Make* Anything Grow, But . . .

We can't make anything grow, but we can foster environments where life *wants to grow.* As I share this revelation, I'm often met with a rebuttal: "Making things grow is the definition of gardening." Truthfully, I cannot disagree more, and if you ask most gardeners, I imagine they'll say the same. Gardeners cannot *make* their plants grow in the way we cannot *force* them to. They have their own will and needs. Gardeners *foster* growth with encouragement, care, and attention to details. You must do the same for yourself.

I hope my thoughts, observations, tools, and stories can help you address your well-being, community, and environment. But I am not the only person who has considered what it means to grow. As you start or continue your path forward, I encourage you to consider the myriad of resources that exist and can aid you. Look into other practices people use around the world for their mind, body, and spirit. Learn from history and the experience of our ancestors. Have conversations with your family, friends, and neighbors. Embrace hobbies, habits, and routines that help you maintain your well-being. Nature has an abundance of resources for us, and its history and wisdom are as old as time. Listen to yourself and your intuition—maybe you'll discover something new.

And, if you feel yourself losing your peace, getting off balance, or out of harmony, remember to stop, take a deep breath, put your hands in some soil, and plant your feet on the earth.

ACKNOWLEDGMENTS

It's hard to believe my first book comes to an end! Writing this book is the result of years of studying, contemplating, taking notes, and of course, great friends, family, and help. I would not be in a position to make this work without the incredible people in my life, whom I must thank for their support and encouragement.

The first thanks must go to Mother Bridgewater. My entire life you have told me that I would be a speaker and a writer. You knew long ago and have always believed in me, never once losing faith. You are a magical being whose heart is unmatched, filled with love and kindness. I am blessed to have that presence in my life. Your support through this entire journey has been unwavering and persistent. Thank you for your integral role in my growth.

Grandma Pearl, Mother Mason, my dearest friend. I knew from the moment I "ran away" and snuck into your house that I was home because I was with you. The strength, determination, and forgiveness you embody has taught me to be kind, patient, and positive. I never had reason to question the idea of "strong women" because I watched you time and time again stand your ground and defend your land against bullets with nothing but a broom in your hand. Thank you for adopting us into your family.

Uncle Sonny, Eugene Mason, thank you for showing me such an honorable example of sacrifice. You gave up a career and entire lifestyle to come home and take care of your family. I have never forgotten that and admire your dedication and love.

Michael, my father, I have yet to meet another man who can speak with such articulation and fervor, let alone in multiple languages. You showed me intellect and gave me a standard to strive for, and I know my gift of words comes from you. It is no surprise you're such a decorated academic. I'm grateful for the depths of our conversations, and I look forward to what the future holds for us.

Aunt Jb, you have always been a fan of mine, giving me continuous encouragement. Your high energy and radiant smile inspire me when I feel myself beginning to frown, and I look forward to the next time I can see you.

Uncle Wilbert, in the few times I have been fortunate enough to share your company, you showed me a divine love for nature and respect for the temples that are our bodies. You also showed me love without judgment. We may not see each other often, but I think of you and your lessons daily. Until the next time, Uncle; bless.

Nancy and David, my wonderful "plant parents," I cannot thank you enough for bringing me into your family at a young age. You set an example of intelligence early on and I continue to soak up knowledge from your abundance of wisdom. Few things make me happier than having more time to visit home and spend time with you. It is fitting that you would give me those original houseplants years ago and spark this journey for me. I love you more than the carambola tree fruits!

Rugerio, you presented me with the opportunity to challenge myself and practice my potential. Porro, you rekindled my love of reading and helped me realize I could be "smart," too. Together, your training helped me become a leader and inspired me to become a teacher.

To the McDonalds, Masons, Bushes, Constants, Griffins, Jemisons, McNeils, Mylonakises, Chapmans, Albrechts, Dailys, Targetts, Demonicos, Chzsanowskis, Nutters, Reddicks, Thomases, and Hammarstroms, my Texas and Florida families and friends—thank you for giving me shelter, food, love, and care when I needed it most.

T-Men, my incredible students: You made teaching

rewarding and fulfilling. Thank you for your hard work, dedication to our craft, and your curiosity to learn. You challenged me in ways that forced me to become a better person and I learned a lot by watching you grow into the awesome people you are today.

My brothers, what adventures we have had together. Your friendship, support, advice, and bright spirits have illuminated my path when darkness took over again and again. Thank you for believing in me when many thought I had nothing to offer but crazy ideas about improving well-being. I am proud of the men we have grown into and look forward to what's to come.

My sisters, thank you for your love and support, and for giving me the insight I needed when I couldn't understand love and ladies.

My thanks to the Fathers at the monastery for letting me live and learn among you. You gave me a place to heal in time of need and find peace in the tranquility of your grounds. A special thanks to Father Isaac for your wisdom and example of selflessness.

To my islands family—thank you for your support over the years. We may not have grown up together, but I'm thankful that the love between us has been strong nonetheless.

To the many lost brothers and sisters of both my families and friends who supported and encouraged me along my way: I think of you often and miss you dearly.

Acknowledgments

To the team who helped me make this work a reality: Toby Mundy, my fantastic agent! You truly are like a literary fairy godfather. You entered my life with cosmic timing, when I was at a crossroads and needed guidance. Within a month, I secured this book deal and my life completely changed in unanticipated ways. Not only are you skilled at what you do, but I leave every conversation with you beaming, cheeks hurting from my smile, and in high spirits. Working with you is great fun and I am thrilled to have had you by my side during this process.

Anna Paustenbach, my editor at HarperOne, you understood my vision for this book from the beginning. Thank you for helping me make it a reality. You saw the potential for this book, and I still cannot believe how fortunate I am to have had your insight and guidance throughout this process. Every note and idea you shared helped bring this work to the next level and for that I am forever grateful. I did not know what to expect when I entered the world of book writing, but you made this process enjoyable, exciting, and genuine. It is a blessing to have had the opportunity to work with you.

Thank you to the HarperOne team for your hard work and expertise. Your dedication to quality and substance is of the highest professional standard I could imagine. This book is a work of art thanks to all of you. Special thanks to Judith Curr for your kindness and support.

Ned, my lawyer, I could not have made it this far without your generous assistance (and potentially losing my mind from contract review). You saw the value in my work immediately and encouraged me to aim high with my goals. You helped me achieve far more than I could have otherwise in my first year of running my business full-time, and on top of that, you made it fun! I look forward to visiting your garden up north and getting my hands dirty with you and the family.

Thank you, Blair, for your timely advice and internet insight. Your support and friendship are invaluable and helped make this book possible.

Last but far from least, my partner and best friend, Dana: You catalyzed this journey for me. You listened and were interested in what I had to say, and what I shared with you was nothing new. I'd shared the same information before but you heard something in my words and offered to help me make a living out of them. I never would have referred to myself as "Garden Marcus" without your suggestion. This book would not exist without you, your patience, and your ability to take my thoughts and weave them into paragraphs. I could write many pages thanking you alone and outlining my appreciation for you, but I know you do not think it's worth the trees it would take to do so. So know this: I love you.